Twelfth
emories

A Collection
of Short Stories

News Letter 🌰

Twelfth Memories - A Collection of Short Stories

ISBN: 978-0-9549715-9-5

News Letter ❀

2 Esky Drive, Carn, Portadown, BT63 5YY

Published in conjunction with the
Grand Orange Lodge of Ireland and Belfast Orangefest.

THE Twelfth is a very special time for many News Letter readers and every year we look for ways to develop and improve our coverage of the famous parades that are renowned the world over.

When the idea of a short story competition came along, we were very keen and we were delighted to co-operate with the Orange Order in making it happen.

While we believed that it would capture the imaginations of our readers, I don't think anyone anticipated what a huge success the competition would become.

We were inundated with entries from across Northern Ireland and even further afield, as people took the chance to commit some of their most cherished memories to print. The standard of writing was incredibly high - some stories captured the colour and pageantry of the "big day", while others brought out the humour and focused on some of the characters encountered in days gone by. A poignant theme ran through many contributions as readers reflected on friends and loved ones with whom they shared a Twelfth and who were no longer with them.

It was a very difficult task choosing winners and there were many lively debates among the judging panel. In the end, the top story was a powerful and moving account of Nigel Lutton's last Twelfth with his father, who was murdered by the IRA.

A selection of the stories was printed in a special News Letter supplement, which proved very popular, and now we are pleased to offer the public the chance to enjoy even more Twelfth experiences from the "bygone days of yore".

Darwin Templeton, Editor, News Letter

Grand Master for Twelfth Memories

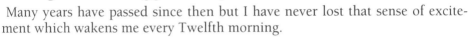

I am delighted to have been asked to write the foreword for this collection of Twelfth Memories, published by the News Letter.

The Twelfth is a huge day in our cultural calendar and my own memories go back to when I was a young boy of 12 in Belfast, watching and then taking part in the parades.

Many years have passed since then but I have never lost that sense of excitement which wakens me every Twelfth morning.

It is a day when we celebrate much that is important to the Reformed Faith and our Protestant heritage. It is a day when we meet old friends and make new ones. We enjoy good music and all the sights and sounds that come with such a huge event.

Surely, there is no other public event in the United Kingdom that can bring such huge numbers of people onto the streets to enjoy the parades, either by taking part in them or simply to watch them go by.

I am proud to lead this great institution and I have been privileged to have taken part in parades all over Northern Ireland and further afield.

Each of us will have our own special memories of the Twelfth, perhaps of loved ones who are no longer with us, of fun packed days and of days that renew our Christian faith.

The News Letter has done a great service by producing this book and the people who have written their stories should also be congratulated on sharing them with us.

There are deeply sad stories, humourous stories and tales of the colour, sound and spectacle of the Twelfth.

It is an incredible day and I am sure that this book will bring back many memories of the Twelfth and at the same time help us re-affirm our determination that it must continue to grow and develop.

Robert Saulters, Grand Master

Twelfth Day

There is always something special about the 'Twelfth Day' – No matter what time the alarm clock rings you are never tired, despite only retiring as the dancing flames of the bonfires give way to smouldering embers. No matter how hard the Belfast summer may fall from the skies, your spirits are never dampened because it never rains on the 'Twelfth', at least not in the memory. The 'Twelfth' is one of those occasions where the senses are sharpened and otherwise insignificant details and normal actions become seared into one's memory banks. How come? - some might ask. After all it is only walking, waving to some friends, having a sit in a park and dandering home again, all set against a background of music. That may be the mechanics, but in the context of tradition, family and faith the 'Twelfth' Day takes on a persona of its own.

The memories that are forged around the experience, whether you are one of the brethren on parade; in the crowds that line the footpath or resplendent in your band uniform, become milestones in the mind, which as the years progress are recalled with pride and affection. Belfast Orangefest seeks to ensure this and the next generation enjoy the same traditional experiences and happy memories of their fathers and forefathers. However, Orangefest are not only committed to safeguarding the integrity of the event and maximising the visual and fun-filled experience of the day, we seek to ensure that memories are created for all who watch the event, especially the increasing number of visitors to our city.

We were delighted to partner the News Letter in the 'Twelfth Memories' competition as we captured and shared with others, what to the Orange family is self evident, the significance of the 'Twelfth' Day. May all enjoy this collection of stories of a day that is played out not only on the streets of Belfast and beyond, but in the hearts and memories of countless thousands.

Tom Haire, Chairman, Belfast Orangefest

Contents Twelfth Memories

The Sash his Father Wore

On the 12th July 1978 excitement filled the air as my mother woke me early so my father and I could get a good breakfast before we headed off to the small Orange Hall in Canary, home of LOL 1287.

My father was already dressed as I ran to the kitchen to devour my cornflakes, I ate them as fast as I could and ran back to my room to find my Sunday clothes and my sash. The small blue sash I wore was given to me by an old man Robbie Murdoch, a lifetime friend of our family whose ancestors had all been Orangemen. A fact of which he was very proud.

On the 11th night I had gone with my father and another older LOL 1287 member to the Argory Estate to pick up a Lambeg drum my father had been repairing inside the old estate's workshop. The air of excitement was in the atmosphere on the 11th night as bands and drums could be heard in the distance practising for the next day.

Pictured in front of the Lambeg drum with my father and his lodge, 12th July 1978

With breakfast over I ran into the yard as my mother insisted on taking a photograph of us before we set out. When this was done I tugged my father towards the car as I wanted to get to the Orange Hall where I knew I would be showered with free brown lemonade and pocket money. When we arrived the Orangemen were already tightening up the Lambeg drums and their noise was deafening. My favourite one had a portrait of King William on it and I stood mesmerised in front of it as the old man playing it swayed from side to side, beating out a double time rhythm.

On this occasion a lifelong member of 1287 was being presented with a 50 year certificate and a special photograph was commissioned to be taken that morning. It was only years later that I realised the picture would mean more to me than the old man's family.

As the lodge lined up for the photograph my father helped to organise the men into rows so we could get ready to move off towards the bus which would bring us to the main parade. As the men lined up I ran to the King William drum which meant the most to me and kneeled in front of it waiting for the picture to be taken. Another young boy there that day also insisted on sitting beside me as it were, at King William's feet.

Soon we were on our way and the bus moved off. The old men sang Orange songs. One old man in particular with a good voice, although crackly as he ran out of breath, sang the Aghalee Heroes, a song which has been one of my favourites ever since. The rest of the day was full of excitement and wonder as I watched people who had been affected by the Troubles on a daily basis suddenly forget the murder and mayhem and enjoy their big day out.

When the bus returned home we walked towards the Argory Estate and the small Canary hall surrounded by trees. At the hall the RUC, who had guarded the hall all day to ensure our safety, suddenly relaxed and they came in for tea. The RUC officers took turns at guarding the porch as we ate our dinner.

I stayed late at the hall that Twelfth as my friend and I hammered the Lambeg unsuccessfully trying to make a tune. As a seven year old the noise I made sounded impressive to me but not to the old men who looked on and laughed in amusement.

My father was one of the last to leave; he took me by the hand, picked up his sash and gloves, as we headed for the car. I waved frantically at the men from the open window of my father's car as they locked up the hall already looking forward to next year, the 12th 1979.

The 12th 1979 came, I was not with Canary LOL 1287 and neither was my father as Sinn Fein/IRA had in May 1979 ambushed and murdered him as he left his work at the Argory close to his home and beside Canary Orange Hall. On the 12th 1979 I was with my grandfather WG Wright at his Orange Lodge Derrycorry Purple Guards LOL 52.

That year as my grandfather took me by the hand into his hall I knew it was time for this eight year old to wear the "Sash his father wore".

Nigel Lutton - Winning Story

Belfast Memories of the Twelfth

There are eight children in our family, four boys and four girls. At the 'Twelfth' mum and dad would take us into Belfast, usually to McMurrays in North Street or some shop on either the Shankill Road or Sandy Row and rig us all out. We got everything from a vest and pants to a new coat and shoes.

About a week before the Twelfth, we would go round all the arches. On the eleventh we would go round the bonfires and on the Twelfth we would get up early and dad would go to the band room, if he was still in the Woodvale pipe band, or to the Orange Hall or the Master's house if he was in the lodge.

We would go with mum to see the bands, sometimes she would take us to the field. It was quite a walk after we got into Belfast city centre, and she would usually have a couple of kids in a big pram and the rest of us hanging on to her skirt. That was in the days before the boys joined the junior lodge and were able to walk in the parade as string boys. They loved to do this because they got paid a few shillings.

When we got to the field there would be vans selling ice cream, burgers, toys etc. and we would spend the few pence we had, usually on something that would be broken before we got home. Then we would sit on a rug on the grass and listen to the bands practising and watch in awe as people, young and old would wander around in band uniforms or suits and bowler hats and white gloves and eat our sandwiches and drink tea from plastic cups.

The field would be strewn with various items belonging to the lodges and banners would be unfurled and propped against a hedge or van. Band instruments would be sitting in groups and usually some wee lad would be banging a drum for all he was worth, much to the amusement of his parents and the annoyance of everyone else sitting within earshot. Then it would be time for the marchers to line up ready for the long march home and we would set off in the hope of getting a bus into town to meet our connecting bus out home to Rathcoole.

Alice Anderson, Belfast

Portglenone to Canada and back

A few years ago, as I was in the field at the Twelfth demonstration in Portglenone, two men were standing in front of me chatting. One with a white cap. I knew him as he came over from Canada every year for the Twelfth of July.

The other man that was standing with him, asked him if he knew anyone from Portglenone. He said the only man he knew from Portglenone was a man that he went over in the boat to Canada with in 1937 and he named him. Just then a man reached past me and tapped the man on the shoulder, and said that he was the man named. He left Canada and spent the rest of the years in America. He also came home every year for the Twelfth. What excitement there was for some time as they talked about the way they went out on the same boat as young men and went their separate ways.

Now they were well up in years, and would not have recognised each other only for the way that the chat was overheard. A lifetime had passed and I thought it was great the way that they had met up that day in the field at the Twelfth demonstration at Portglenone and renewed their friendship. I loved to see the man from Canada every time he came home. I asked him all about Canada and he would tell all about his time out there. Both men have since passed on, at a good age.

The platform party at the Field on the Twelfth

Anna Carleton, Portgelone

Recollection of Twelfth as a teenager in the 40s

My family lived less than eight miles from Londonderry - nowadays a 10 minute journey by car. Then it seemed we were in the heart of Donegal - a long way from the city - and having to cross the border made it seem even more distant. Coming from a farming background, without electricity, dependent on the horse, life seemed to be of a very rural nature - and we would be known as 'Country Gabs'.

My brother Samuel was a member of Newtowncunningham LOL 1066, while my brothers Albert and Tom were pipers with the band.

During June/July my brothers would practice on the chanter, later they would march along our lane playing the bagpipes. The skirl could be heard for miles around on a quiet summer evening. There were not many tractors or heavy machinery around to dull the sound. No interference with headphones, mobile phones, no house phones. Come to think of it there was no television just the wireless with its dry battery.

The band tutor was a Mr. Cruikshanks from Creggan in the city (Yes, Protestants lived in Creggan in those days). He would arrive at the hall on his motorbike. Sadly he lost his life in a road accident on his way home one evening.

The tunes 'Shall We Gather at the River', 'Abide With Me', 'Onward Christian Soldiers' and others were well rehearsed. The boys would set off on their bikes to the state. It would be quite tricky juggling the bagpipes on the bike - which wouldn't always have sound brakes - the side of the shoe might have to be held firmly against the front tyre to slow things down.

At last the big day arrived - the uniforms spic and span - the skirts having been laid out on the box hedge at our front door to air, this was possibly to rid them of the smell of mothballs. The tunics would be hung in the kitchen on hangers - the sporran well brushed - socks. Glengarry all now in good order it was time to meet at the Hall.

Outside the Hall a private bus (L & LSR) was waiting. People would be standing around; the pipes could be heard being tuned up by Albert who was now Pipe Major.

Soon the banner was brought out and unfurled - Brethren would raise it up into the leather pouch worn from the shoulder, the streamers would be carried by young people. The big drum decorated with Sweet William and Orange Lillies was brought out, the side drummers and pipers all would line up, the leader David McClean, tall and straight (I think wearing a Busby) ready.

Names like Roulston, Watson, Orr, Smyth, Woods, Devenney, King, Robb, McBride, Hoey, Sproule, McClintock, Gibson, Piper, Williamson, come to mind (there were others).

Soon they were on their way, parading to the bottom of the street and back before boarding the bus for a good day out. This exercise was repeated on their return in the evening - foot sore and weary.

I am reminded of a photograph in the Derry Journal (1947) showing a very wet and bedraggled parade marching down Carlisle Road, the caption 'Ranting In The Rain'.

Sadly time and change brought the inevitable, but I am filled with pride when I see a young and vibrant Accordion Band from Newtowncunningham strutting their stuff on the Twelfth.

Long may they 'Rant In The Rain' or better still sunshine.

Anna Molloy, Londonderry

My Twelfth Story

I have very happy memories of the Twelfth of July in Co Fermanagh. During the war years the Twelfth was not held but I do remember after the war one Twelfth morning someone came to our house at 6.30am asking for my father to go and fife for the Lambeg drums that were taking out a local lodge.

We lived on a farm in Roslea and our Catholic neighbours came and looked after the farm on that day and in return my father did the same on their day, 15th August. When I was about 10 years old and the eldest of the family I remember going to the Twelfth with my father. We travelled as far as the local lodge about six miles away in our pony and trap. There the pony was stabled at a farm and we all got on a milk lorry with wooden benches and travelled to the nearest Twelfth demonstration in Newtownbutler. The ladies of the lodge looked after me whilst my father went on parade with his lodge. He was called the lone fifer and played along with the Lambeg drums, which have rhythm only, but my father always kept in tune and that was his pride and joy.

As we were a large family, my mother stayed at home with the younger children and they got a treat of ice cream and brown lemonade. Then for dinner they would have had new potatoes freshly dug from the field. I have such happy childhood memories of the Twelfth. I now tell my grandchildren all the stories of those days 60 years ago.

Anna Watson, Monea, Co. Fermanagh

The Sash my Father Wore

MY MEMORIES flashed back to the 1950s. The Twelfth had arrived. Everyone seemed to be rushing around getting ready.

My father, grandfather and uncle were all called McCracken and all belonged to the Ballykeel Orange Lodge in the Holywood Hills. They all seemed to be dressed in dark navy suits, white shirts and navy tie, black shoes, white gloves and the most important part of dress was the orange sash.

Off they went to walk to meet at the Orange Hall. Mother called 'Here comes the taxi for us'.

There was granny, my mother, my sister Eileen, myself and our neighbours the Pattersons.

Off we went with our food baskets of corned beef and spam sandwiches with fruit cake. Rugs and raincoats were all piled into the taxi.

At first we arrived in Holywood at the field, across the gate was a big banner 'Welcome Brethren'. We found a nice spot under some trees. We all chatted to neighbours that we had not seen for a long time. In the field were tents, the churches had tea stalls with books, toys, china and tablecloths. There were hobby horses for us children and book stalls.

We always had a lovely poke of ice-cream with lots of raspberry. Every child had a small Union Jack to wave. At last someone yells "Here they come."

Well, this was what we had been all waiting for. The first lodge appearance. The banner swaying in the wind a portrait usually of a Master of the Lodge with a line of a Scripture verse across the banner.

The pipe bands, the skirl of the pipes and the echo of the drums over the fields and hills. A big long line of Orange banners all lovely and lodges with flute and brass bands. Then came the Lambegs. I always put my hands over my ears until they passed.

King Billy was always astride a big white horse dressed in a big hat with a black curly wig and a blue tunic and big long black boots with swords.

At last, Ballykeel Orange Lodge and Flute Band. We know most of the men but we all

Pictured in the centre with my granda and great uncle McCracken. My father and uncle are in the back row. My mother, sister Eileen and two Patterson brothers are also in the photograph.

waved and shouted. Then we saw Daddy carrying the sword. We all called out and waved. Another special person was in the band, the man I married many years later in 1964.

Uncle Tom carrying the banner and Granda carrying a long pole to keep the crowds back.

Well all I can say what a lovely Twelfth we all had. But most of all it seems like only yesterday.

My father was a very tall, quiet man and the Twelfth was very special for him.

He always sang or whistled The Sash My Father Wore. As I looked out this old Orange Sash it brings back fond memories of my father and his religious beliefs.

It is old, but is it beautiful, and the colours they are fine, it was on the Twelfth I loved to wear the Sash my father wore.

Anna Moore, Newtownards

In 1960

Ballykeel Orange Lodge, Co Down

The Sash, The Rain and The Falls Road

BALLYGOMARTIN Temperance LOL No 741 was formed early after the Second World War - warrant taken out in late 1948.

The seven founding members all lived in the Ballygomartin Road area. The lodge met in Clifton Street Orange Hall on the last Wednesday of each month at 7.30pm.

The Orange Lodge from Rutherglen Street preparing for parade on the Twelfth in 1953

I was born in Rutherglen Street on 30th June 1944, the youngest of a large family with a long and honourable tradition in the Woodvale/Ballygomartin Road area. My father, George Whitley, joined Ballygomartin Temperance LOL 741 shortly after its formation and was Worshipful Master in 1953. That is were my memory starts, the late spring/summer of 1953.

I was nine-years-old and attending Forth River School, I was in 2nd standard and my teacher was Mrs Parman. It was already a memorable time with the Stanley Matthews Cup Final in May at Wembley, the conquest of Everest and Queen's Coronation in early June.

My earliest memory is my mother getting a new dress and her hair done. That must have been a few days prior to the 12th. I was taken for a hair cut to Sammy Morton on the Woodvale Road, always a very funny experience for a nine-year-old. Sammy, as they said in the Woodvale, "was a great man in the Welcome Hall in Cambrai Street."

The 11th night was the bonfire located at the junction at the top of Rutherglen Street and Glencairn Street. We had lots of sandwiches, buns and apple pie, certainly the buns and apple pie supplied by O'Hara's - who must have had four Home Bakeries on the Shankill/Woodvale in the early 1950s. Sadly now all are gone. Does anyone now make custards like O'Hara's? I remember being called in at about 9.00 - 9.30 and getting a bath, the large steel bath was taken down from its moorings on a large nail in our back yard and filled with endless pots of hot water. After my bath it was bed in the small 'box room' and I recall feeling very safe and secure between the cool cotton sheets, I listened to the sound of distant Lambeg drums as I slowly drifted off to sleep. I arose the next morning at

6.30am, my Mom and Dad already up. I tucked into an Ulster fry with my mom's words ringing in my ears.... "Eat that up - God knows when you will eat again"... My clothes for the Twelfth were left out on my bed. A new pair of short grey trousers and a grey shirt bought in Loane's on the Shankill Road, a new pair of sandals bought in Brown's on the Crumlin Road - you know I never remember wearing any other footwear as a child - sandals in summer and boots in winter. On this occasion, my debut as a 'string boy' and my first walk to Finaghy I was strongly advised to wear my 'old' sandals.

The day had dawned bright and dry, still I heard somebody say "it's to rain later on". The members of 741 started to arrive at our house from about 7.30am, my father being Master, the Lodge would leave from outside our house. I was to carry the string of the banner and walk to Finaghy for the first time. What sheer joy and pride I felt.

Ballygomartin Temperance LOL 741 did not have a banner, they had borrowed a banner. It would be another two years before they would purchase a banner, with the new Ballygomartin Presbyterian Church on one side. My parents were members of Ballygomartin Presbyterian Church and I had gone to Sunday School since about 3/4-years-old. Something happened..... and I was encouraged to join the Lifeboys in Argyle Place Presbyterian Church (now West Kirk). I was then to progress to 96th Belfast BB Company. That would bring me into contact with two future Presbyterian Ministers - Rev Brian Savage and Rev Brian Kennaway. I would also come under the considerable influence of Rev Robert Dickinson, Robert Savage, Harry Hawthorne, Tommy Stewart and others.

Billy McAreavey at that time owned the 'Eagle' at the corner of Rutherglen Street. He sold a range of sweets and papers. Billy opened early on Twelfth morning and I recall someone gave me a shilling (1/-). I had then, and still have now a great passion for liquorice and I remember going to the 'Eagle' to obtain a vast collection of liquorice for my 1/-.

Just before the lodge moved off the string boys had their photo taken and were given small Orange collarette's (sashes) and also received instructions about holding the string. Our lodge did not have a band so we waited at the corner of Rutherglen Street for another lodge with a band to pass and then fall in behind and progress to Clifton Street to link up with the main parade. My mother and two aunts would take up position on the Lisburn Road just outside the Samaritan Hospital and wave and shout. They would then meet up with us at 'The Field'. I remember getting tired about Adelaide Park on the Lisburn Road and the rest of the walk was a struggle. During our sandwiches and buns at 'The Field', it was decided that I would not do the walk home and would go home with my mother and aunts. We had only walked a couple of hundred yards when dark clouds loomed and the rain came... it was torrential. We were all soaked as we ran for a bus. In those days the bus from 'The Field' must have gone down the Falls Road. I remember the bus was very full with lots of people getting on and off. We all got to Castle Street/Castle Junction. Then amidst great excitement and laugher it was discovered that the small collarette I had worn to carry the string and walk to 'The Field' I had worn down the Falls Road on the bus. This became a family story and a 741 story about "one of the only men to wear a sash down the Falls Road".

There my memory ends of 12th July 1953, except for getting back to our house and a change into warm clothes and a bowl of hot soup. Oh! and I got my 2/6 (two shillings and sixpence) for carrying the string.

Over the years this story would be told and re-told. My mother died in Belfast City Hospital on 25th March 1975, she had been born on 12th April 1900. The day before she died, when clearly a very ill woman, she told me of watching 'boys' going off to the First World War and of the day I went down the Falls Road with my sash on. That raised a laugh. My father died on 12th February 1977, he was born on 25th April 1897. A few days before his death he spoke about enlisting into the 14th Battalion Royal Irish Rifles (YCV) sometime in 1915 at the Scout Hall in Bray Street on the Woodvale. My father then also spoke about the "day you went down the Falls with your sash on". How he laughed. A few days later he died.

That's my memory of a Twelfth long past. When I see one of those small collarettes, experience heavy torrential rain or I am on the Falls Road, I always think of the sash, the rain and the Falls Road and the 12th of July 1953.

Bill Whitley, Dunmurry

My Memories of the Twelfth in the early 1920s

What an exciting time for a wee boy on that important day. Dad brought the horse and vehicle to the front door of our house, loaded mother, sister, myself and our next door neighbour all in our Sunday best at the end of our lane where my school teacher lived, who was not of our faith. She was out to see us off and gave me a half-crown. What a surprise my neighbour also gave me a half-crown it was going to be a great day.

The demonstration was in our local village of Derrygonnelly, mother in her wisdom told me not to spend all my money that day. Oh boy, I was so excited. The village was a picture, bunting went from house to house, the Union Flag was out of the windows in a lot of houses. A friend of dad kept the horse in the yard. Crowds of people were gathered, there were bandsmen and Orangemen everywhere, wee boys and girls like myself were having a great time.

I decided to spend some of my money. I loved the ice-cream and the lemonade, it was a real treat for a cub that did not get too much. What a thrill to watch the banners, bands and the lines of Orangemen in the parade, that was the icing on the cake for me even now in advanced years I still look back and think what a small boy loved.

Bob Abercrombie, Enniskillen

Happy Memories of the Twelfth

Iwas both surprised and slightly apprehensive when asked to lead the Twelfth procession in Maguiresbridge last year. My only experience was at Snowhill Lodge's centenary celebration in 2005 where I made a brief appearance on my white Connemara mare.

New experiences often prove to be fun so I agreed and two days before the occasion I met my foot soldiers who were to walk either side of the horse, and collected my new costume. And what a costume it was! A beautiful dark red velveteen jacket and matching waistcoat trimmed with gold braid and a pure white shirt with huge frilly ruffs. It was lovely, although less could be said for the curly wig. At least I had the choice of a number of hats. I chose the best one which sported a white feather and later caused great mirth at home, as unbeknown to me a white feather is a sign of cowardice. I hoped nobody else would notice.

The day before the Twelfth I scrubbed the white pony with white horse shampoo. It would never do if King William's white charger was dirty. Her saddle and bridle and my boots were polished and to add to the carnival atmosphere I had purchased a red, white and blue traditional wool halter and breastplate with tassels from ebay. This looked just the part.

On the morning of the Twelfth I dressed up as King Billy on his white charger and led Derryclavin the local pipe band (my grandfather had a long association with it) along the main street of our village. The charger was on her toes and pranced and danced along in front of the band, so I took her home and quickly removed the costume and took her for a couple of good sharp canters to take the edge off her.

On returning we loaded her into the horsebox and drove to the Twelfth. We joined the queue and eventually we unloaded in the midst of a throng of people, traffic and bands turning up. I hopped onto her back and away to the church beside the field where the bands were congregating before the march. Here my good little mare stood like a rock while we waited for the off. Lots of children stroked her and said how soft she was, so I told them she had a bath especially for the day. They probably wondered how I got the horse into the bath.

Finally we were off, following a single policeman, making our way slowly through the throng of people who covered the whole roadway. What an experience. We soon lost sight of our policeman as he merged into the crowd.

As we proceeded towards the village we had to cross a bridge and this was the first place were I noticed the cameras. They were above us on the bridge.

As we crossed the bridge and came round the corner into the main street it appeared to be an impenetrable sea of bodies with no way through. Nothing had prepared me for this. It was incredible, helium balloons, flags, fire crackers, streamers, all the colour and movement and so many people. As the foot soldiers, my mount and the band proceeded forward the crowd parted on either side like the waves in the Red Sea in the Bible.

As we neared the end of the street we spied the television cameras on a traffic island in the centre of the road and after this the spectators thinned out and we made our way to the field, where our particular duty ended. We waited and watched the band proceed into the field and then quietly took our leave.

I never thought I would be personally involved in the Twelfth, but I'm glad I was and would not have missed this wonderful and unique experience for anything.

Charmian Goodall, Lisbellaw

Leading the parade at the Twelfth in Maguiresbridge

Memories of the 'Glorious Twelfth'
and Granny's 'Conglomeration' Sandwiches!

IT was 40 years ago almost to the day since, at the tender age of three, I left the leafy, idyllic surroundings of Hazelwood Terrace in the townland of Slaght to move some four miles or thereabouts into the town of Ballymena. Now here I was, on the 12th July 2004 (age 43) standing outside that humble row of red brick terraced factory houses, on a gloriously sunny afternoon, with memories of childhood 'Twelfths' flooding back.

As I reflected on my childhood memories that July afternoon, I was conscious, as I am now, that I might be viewing some of the scenes through rose coloured spectacles. For one thing, in all my nostalgic recollections of the 'Twelfth Day' there is never a cloud in sight. The sun always seems to be splitting the trees, ripening the blackcurrants and gooseberries in my grandmother's garden and only the gentlest of breezes stirs the Union flag fluttering above her front door.

It was granny's home that became the focal point of the day, as the venue for a reunion of our extended family - the only time apart from weddings and funerals when aunts, uncles and cousins made the pilgrimage to granny's cottage on the Toome Road. As I recall, most of our numerous relations made an appearance at some point throughout the day, regardless of whether or not they swore allegiance to the 'Loyal Institution' or adopted a more diluted Orange approach to the festivities!

I can still remember my excitement as I walked down the pathway to granny's house with my four older sisters - the crunch of the gravel under our feet and the first glimpse of granny's old black-framed bike leaning against the gable wall. I remember as if it were yesterday the two Billy goats grazing in the long unkempt grass of her back garden, looking somewhat apprehensive with the approaching beat of the Lambeg drum. Even though as a child I understood little, if anything, of the historical background or political implications associated with the occasion, the first distant beat of that drum and the skirl of the bagpipes had spine-tingling impact.

I remember the great anticipation with which we stood outside Wallace's shop on Henry Street, waiting for our first glimpse of Slaght Lodge 475, its banner fluttering in the summer breeze, the marchers resplendent in their bowlers and Orange regalia, as they made their way over Harryville Bridge. Eagerly we scanned the ranks looking for dad and his lifelong friend Robert, walking side by side as they had done season after season.

The honour of holding the strings was the ultimate thrill for a 10-year-old and my own particular opportunity lives on in my memory. Standing beside those thunderous drums, how I wished I could be the one rattling out 'Kellswater' or 'Cock of the North' with such gusto! Another vivid memory is of the black-suited, sashed and white-gloved Orangemen, calling religiously each Twelfth morning to dress the drums with Orange Lillies and Sweet William from granny's garden. Granny with a mischievous twinkle, would remind the brethren that the flowers they had just plucked were in fact "green when they came out at first!"

Granny Lamont was an Ulster woman by birth, yet Scottish in loyalty and inclination. During the war years she had worked in an ammunitions factory in Glasgow, then later as an orderly at Stobhill Hospital. Hard working and uncompromising, she had a faith that moved mountains. Granny was a gifted storyteller, spinning yarns with such conviction you were compelled to sit up and listen. On our 12th of July reunions we were her captive audience, regaled with endless anecdotes and canny quotes, especially from 'Rabbie Burns!'

Family reunion on the Twelfth day at Granny Lamont's

Some of her stories, to our delight, recalled the childhood misdemeanours of our mother, known in the family as Molly. My poor mother's face reddened with embarrassment, while we all fell about laughing, enjoying her discomfiture.

Despite the scorching hot weather that registers in my memory, there always seemed to be a peat fire glowing in the hearth. The smell of strong tea mingled with the pungent aroma of peat and the 'Ulster fry' with which granda and Aunt Annie began the day - the only way, after all, to start the Twelfth. Annie, our youngest aunt, unmarried and still living at home in those days, seemed to us children incredibly glamorous and avantgarde, sitting by the fireside in her 60s mini-skirt, painting her fingernails. With a tray balanced on one knee and her feet tapping to the sound of Hank Williams playing on the old radiogram, she would holler to granny, "Any more fudge mother, or another slice of soda bread?"

Later in the day, when the processions had passed and all the family had assembled, granny would appear from the scullery with a big plate of sandwiches and her famous home-baked rock buns. "Anyone for a conglomeration sandwich?" she would ask (so named because of the 'conglomeration' of ingredients - tomato, lettuce, ham, cheese, corned beef, eggs, pickles and plenty more forbye!) - a feed that would have choked a donkey.

When Dad and the other Orangemen came trudging home, weary from their walk to the field and back, there were big mugs of tea and more conglomeration sandwiches for everybody. There were platefuls of trifle too and (if you had the stomach for it) glasses of granny's homemade wine (which she always insisted could be drunk without fear of breaking the pledge, although there were those who could give evidence to the contrary). "Granny, you'll be getting fat with all this grub you're eating", someone suggested. "Not me", Granny retorted, "ye cannae fatten a thoroughbred!"

These and many other memories flooded my consciousness on that July afternoon as I stood among the hawthorn hedgerows in the countryside where I had spent so many happy buttercup summers, with the Lambeg drums dunnerin o'er the hills and the prospect of the 'Glorious Twelfth' ahead as the highlight of those sun-filled days.

Colin Agnew, Ballymena

Fond Childhood Memories

Growing up as a wee lad in Portadown I knew what the Twelfth was all about. For me it didn't cross my mind that it brought a certain amount of tension between our communities. For me it was about spending time with my cousins, running around in the field in the sunshine and pretending to be the drummer in a band.

My dad, who was an Orangeman, moved out of the house when I was seven. After that, me and my little sister used to spend a lot of time on my uncle's farm in Stewartstown, Co Tyrone. My aunt and uncle had two children, the same age as me and my sister, so we were always thick as thieves, we still are.

Me and my cousin used to run around the farm together, milking cows, feeding pigs, dunging out the cattle sheds and generally getting up to no good. We had great times in Stewartstown as a kid.

When we were about ten, we worked out a scam of getting paid twice on a Saturday. After working ourselves into the ground all day, my uncle used to pay us a fiver at tea time as we walked down the yard towards the big farm house for our supper. After tea, my uncle's father, also a farmer, came to the house to sit in front of the big open fire for the evening. He used to produce our wages as well, another fiver each. We never let on.

All these memories are vivid but the clearest memories I have in Stewartstown are of the Twelfh of July celebrations.

The anticipation started building a day or two before the parade as the bunting only went up in the village a couple of days before the parade. Sunshine, red, white and blue bunting and plenty of flags. The silver band were practising in the Orange Hall at the top of the hill and the Orangemen were milling around making final preparations for their annual big day out.

On the 11th night the arguing started. I was brought up in the town and my cousins were brought up in the country. This meant that on the Twelfth, I wanted to wear jeans and a t-shirt but my aunt wanted me to wear a shirt and tie. This was alien to me but after a lot of shouting and stomping I always agreed to put on a tie to look as smart as my cousin. A good supper and early to bed.

I never slept much on the 11th night. I was always lying thinking about the next day. Would I get to carry a flag at the front of the band or would I get to hold the rope in front of the banner or would we miss out this year? The morning came quickly and after a good breakfast and a bit more stalling, we put on our shirts and ties and headed down to the hall with my uncle. The excitement nearly bursting out of our ears, the adrenaline pumping so hard that we couldn't sit still.

We made it, we were first and as I was asked to hold a rope from the lodge's banner it was a proud moment for a young boy. For the next two hours the banner was not let out of my sight in case some other country kid muscled in and stole my place. The drummers practised, the fluters tinkered away and all the uniforms were checked over.

A quick cup of tea and the band and Orangemen formed up. Proudly at the front were me and my cousin holding the ropes as if it was the most important job in the world. For that day, it was.

As the July sun shone down I wished I had a t-shirt on. I looked smart though and as we walked through the village I heard my name being called three or four times my mum, granny and granda, great aunt Violet, my auntie, my sister all making me feel proud, proud like a man should feel. The music was wonderful, drums, flutes, pipes, cymbals, trumpets, trombones, all adding to the flavour of the day.

Ice cream was devoured in the field and that was before we had our chicken sandwiches and a bottle of warm, fizzy orange. We ran around without a care in the world, talking to people we knew, thumping drums, eyeing up girls, oblivious to the speeches and boring adult conversations taking place around us.

A few hours later, we had dragged our short weary legs back through the village, stood there tired and bored as the band and marchers formed out and finished off their conversations, maybe not seeing each other, some of them, until the following summer.

As we piled out of the car and into the house, there was a lot less chat than on the way. We were hungry and needed our batteries recharged for the annual after Twelfth celebrations of our own around the farmyard.

When all the food was eaten and all the dishes were washed and put away, a magical transformation happened. Saucepans became drums, lids became cymbals, wooden spoons became flutes, and the flag from the back of the house was taken off the wall.

We put hats on our heads and our ties back on. I carried the flag and held it as high as I could. My cousin Brian became the lead snare with a saucepan tied round his neck with a bit of old rope. The girls were dummy fluters of course.

As the sun set behind the back hills, we paraded around and around and around the yard until we nearly dropped. It was the end of a perfect day and a fond childhood memory.

Dave Wiggins, Portadown

To the Field and Back

For years there have been peaceful and colourful processions without harm, hurt or offence to any man. The mode of the marches may have changed somewhat, but the make up and the humour remains the same. This is my account of walking to the field as a string boy in 1955, a few years before I joined the Institution as a senior Brother in 1962.

It's a long time ago since I first walked to the Field, but over those years, the craic and the banter has remained much the same. My first outing was as a string boy with my da's lodge and in those days the yearly walk went to Finaghy, in south Belfast. Unfortunately it rained cats and dogs that day and everyone was fairly soaked to the skin - that's me (aged 11) in the centre of the photograph wearing the long pacamac.

The road to the field, 1955

However the build-up for each walk would always be the same and more especially for an over excited youngster.

Lack of sleep after the eleventh night dancing round the bonfire and what was left of a sleepless night, looking forward to what the dawn would bring .. the many lodges and bands parading on the Twelfth.

So up with the lark and with the face scrubbed and the hair slicked back with water and the ankle boots polished that you practically could see your face in them, you fell in along with your da to go to the Worthy Master's house for assembly. We always looked a right pair walking up the street.

Me like a choirboy and the da like something out of Burton's window with the Sunday best retrieved out of Joe Tougher's pawn for the next few days, before it was pledged back in again.

At the Master's house the usual refreshments were handed out, mixed minerals for the banner boys and a drop of the harder stuff for the grown ups .. as if they hadn't got enough the night before. Or as the da would say 'it was only to whet the whistle'. More than likely it was a starter for the rest of the day!!

Eventually the band and lodge paraded up to meet with the other lodges in Clifton Street prior to the 'march off' to the field, which was in those days situated on Finaghy Road North at the top of the upper Lisburn Road.

Along the route there would be the usual banter from the on-lookers; the crowds; the families and friends. When the Ballymacarrett district came along, the usual cry was 'come on the Blues' from the Linfield supporters to the 'wise men from the east' .. in rival Glentoran country, who always retorted with a slogan about the 'cock 'n hens'.

Or as the West Belfast No. 9 District Lodge passed, the singing of 'we're the people of the Shankill Road' would echo along Royal Avenue.

Some of the banter to visiting Scots brethren invariably referred to what they wore under their kilts. The usual one about the band who travelled every year to walk on the Twelfth brought this quip from one spectator .. 'ye see them uns, they've been walking here about twenty odd years'.. with the response, 'Gawd they must be tired walking for that length of time!

The brightly coloured Union Jack dresses worn by the dancing ladies who yearly gathered there, outside the old Grand Central Hotel was a joy to behold. At the end of the day they must have covered the distance to the field and back several times due to the amount of dancing they had done. They certainly inspired many a youngster who even at that early stage in the parade had already, a pair of sore feet. I've heard it sung many a time that it's a long way to Tipperary, the walk to the Field seemed even longer.

The humour itself was typical of Ulster people. When the crowd spilled onto the road there was always one lig who would shout... "Get back ye buck eejits, ye'd think you were all kitchen house reared."

Or to a big burly policeman who would stop at the wrong spot and block the view of the onlookers .. 'if you were a pain of glass we'd see through ye, but yer not big fella, wud ye not go and park somewhere else'. Usually the banter was enough to move him along .. with a brightly red face'.

A tired wee boy reached a distant field in mid afternoon, but getting the packed lunch from the church caterers and an ice cream was always happily received as well as the green grass that made a comfortable seat before the long trek back.

However having covered the walk there, the return journey always seemed shorter for some reason. Could it be that at the end of the day it would be a half crown beckoning for the boys who had carried the string of the banner?

Or was it the fact that once again free minerals and sandwiches or maybe a packet of crisps were on the menu at the Master's house or perhaps that half crown to be spent in Walter Chambers' wee toy shop on the Shankill?

Whatever the reason it was sad that the Twelfth day would soon be over for another year and 12 months can be a long time to wait for a very impatient kid.

Those days were the happiest in my life, like many other kids from the area, marching on the Twelfth with your da's lodge. Unfortunately he now parades with the great Grand Lodge in the heavens above, with me taking the place where the 'ould fella' used to be.

The lodge is still the same however and whatever mother nature has to offer in the evolution of life, some things still have to carry on and the Orange Lodge is one of them. It has been part of many a family for past generations and 'God willing' will continue to be so for the foreseeable future. Orange to some may be a colour .. to us it's a way of life!!

Bro. Ed Spence LOL 1892, Belfast

Memories of the Twelfth

AS children we looked forward to the Twelfth of July with excitement and anticipation. A new dress and white ankle socks was something to look forward to as well as the few delicacies that we enjoyed. It was the war years when little was much appreciated and luxuries were few.

Strawberries were a novelty usually available because they were grown locally. I recall walking up Clogher Street, punnet of strawberries in hand, and an old lady sat in her dilapidated doorway. I passed her the strawberries and looking up in bewilderment she said: "Child dear I'm a Catholic." Hardly knowing what she meant, I said: "But don't you like strawberries?" reluctantly she did have a few then began searching through a deep pocket in her long black apron for a coin. I explained I had a few shillings left, so with a gentle tap on the head and 'God bless you child' I said goodbye.

A very warm Twelfth in Donemana circa 1982

The colourful display of bands following in rotation depicting a fabulous event once seen always remembered.

As children we often had the privilege of carrying the banner strings. Never did we complain about the long walk.

Then tea in the field with the Orangemen and a welcome rest. All too soon the great celebration of William crossing the Boyne had passed.

Another Twelfth ebbed to a close. The memories linger, friendship renewed another year for old and young alike.

Many a lasting relationship was made on the Twelfth.

The national anthem sung, goodbyes said it was home again to help on the farm. To God above we gave praise, now and evermore lest we forget the memory of King William crossing the Boyne.

Frances Gibson, Omagh

Sons and Daughters
of King James

Many, many years ago, in the late Forties, when we were children our uncle and aunt and their family called with us on their way home from the Twelfth.

What would our cousins and we play on the Twelfth evening? 'Wee bands' of course!!!

Using a Union flag we attached it to another rod to make a banner. A toy drum, and combs with paper were all that we needed to make music and parade around the yard.

What to call our band? Our Local Lodge - then Corlea - but now Gillygooley LOL 339 had on their banner the title 'Sons of William', but we declared that we were the sons and daughters of James.

We could not understand why our parents were so amused, for after all, both our fathers were called James.

Mrs Eileen M. Hammond, Omagh

The Excitement of the Twelfth

AT long last school's finished for the summer! You know once you got to the last day of school you started to get really excited. You knew that you would be getting new clothes, you always got new clothes for the 12th of July. My earliest memories of the July holiday, the excitement of collecting bonfire wood and the noise of the bands.

The bonfire didn't look like a bonfire until a few days before the 11th of July, but the collecting of the wood started weeks before this. Sometimes when you went home your mum would ask 'If you've been down the mines digging for coal'. At that time you didn't really understand what she was on about, cause all you had been doing was collecting wood.

Once school was finished for the summer you got to stay out late to look after the wood (because other parts of the estate would come and nick your wood to make their fire bigger than yours), huts would be built and the older kids would stay up all night to protect our wood. Then the day would arrive when we could start to build our bonfire (it could take days just to get it right). You hoped that your fire would be bigger than last years, although when you are small everything looks big and it really seemed if you climbed to the top of the fire you could touch the sky. The last thing to go on our fire was the flag, then we had to wait until it got dark, but it seemed to take forever to get dark.

Mums and dads got tables and chairs from their houses, made a big line so all the kids could have a street party - juice, sweets, games and music, and the parents had their own special drink which we weren't allowed to have.

Then it started to get dark, a small bonfire was always built for the wee kids, they usually fell asleep before the big one was lit.

You knew the time was getting closer when everyone started to move towards the bonfire. It was usually a dad who would light the fire. He went round and round the fire with a petrol can, and bottles were thrown at the top so that it would catch fire. The big fire is lit at 12 midnight on the dot. The dads would light rags or paper and throw it onto the fire. The smoke starts, then a small flicker of a flame (sometimes it would take a second or third attempt especially if it rained during the day) and as it slowly grows bigger and bigger everyone starts to cheer as it reaches the top, the sky lights up and you have to move back from the flames because it's so warm, then it's time to go home and even though it was late you still have to get your bath so you were clean to go and watch the bands.

It seems like you've only closed your eyes and the noise of the bands woke you up, (bands came from everywhere). It's time to get up, put your new clothes on and go watch the bands.

We usually went to Carlisle Circus/Royal Avenue, you had to fight your way through the crowds, bands and the lodge men. If you found a space at the front then you stayed there otherwise you lost your spot. We would stand for hours and hours and watch the bands go by, waving flags and watching out for uncles and shout out their names but with the noise of the bands they never heard you. If you were lucky you had your own wee drum. When the last band went past it was time to go home and wait and wait for the bands to come back from the field.

Elaine Prynne, Belfast

Twelfth Memories

An invitation card sent over 100 years ago to our family from Lavin LOL 913

ONE Twelfth that I have lasting memories of took place about 70 years ago. It was in the village of Castledawson, Co. Londonderry. I was about eight years of age and my brother who was two years older went with me into the village on the Twelfth morning to watch the two local Lodges, LOL 96 and 97 do their customary parade around the town before boarding the train that would take them to the venue. After their departure we would normally have returned home or gone off to the woods or the castle farmyard to help out with odd jobs, so if we didn't turn up at home mother wouldn't have worried.

Well we didn't return home but found ourselves on the train, how I do not know. As we were among people we knew we didn't worry.

That particular Twelfth was being held in Coleraine and included lodges from all of Co. Londonderry.

The train stopped at all the stations on the way to Coleraine to pick up more Lodges, ie Magherafelt, Knockloughrim, Maghera, Upperlands, Kilrea, Garvagh, before joining the Main Line at Mackin.

We duly arrived in Coleraine, a long way from home for two very young boys without a penny in our pockets, but my brother knew if we stayed close with the Lodge we should be okay. How we got through the day I don't remember.

It was only in later years when I went to work in Coleraine that memories of places came back to me such as the Station Square etc. I think the parade was to a field in the Carthall area.

The one lasting memory that I do remember vividly was on the return journey home. I had got into the railway carriage 'non corridor' and was sitting next to the window, the carriage door was open as people piled in and my right hand was holding the opening where the hinges are when someone pulled the door shut.

I can still feel the pain when I think about it today.

Suddenly I was showered with sweets and drinks to stop me crying.

This all happened a long time ago but I still have the indent running the full length of my forefinger nail to remind me of the Twelfth when two little brothers went for an adventure.

Gerald Bradley, Portstewart

A Truly Glorious Twelfth

To most of the people of north Antrim, 12th July 1986 was no more memorable than any other Twelfth. If asked, one who was there might comment that the demonstration was held in Ballycastle and that it was a dry day. To me, however, it was the most glorious of all Twelfths up until then and, even today, it was a special day indeed.

O'Haras True Blues LOL 804 had existed in the village of Bendooragh, near Ballymoney, since the early part of the nineteenth century. The lodge had survived at least seven monarchs and two World Wars but sadly the Orange Hall in the centre of the village had been vacated in 1971 and the lodge collapsed in 1973. I have only one blurred memory of the old lodge yet my grandfather wore his blue collarette complete with the number 804 until his death in 1978 even though his adopted lodge wore orange sashes. With him died the colour blue and the number 804 so long associated with Bendooragh.

Years later, as a 17 year-old, I joined childhood friends in a clean up of the old hall. The roof had caved in, the windows and doors had lost the war with woodworm and rot and the ground around it was a jungle of briars and unchecked hedges. We worked hard all that summer to restore the tarnished pride of the Orange Hall and, after some weeks, the briars were gone, the roof was patched and the fence had been mended. It was then that someone suggested re-opening the old lodge. For a time it was much talked about but not acted on, chiefly because none of us knew what to do! Of my peers, I was the only one who had, at that time, joined the Orange Order but as a very junior member, I was clueless!

At the next lodge meeting I attended, I asked our lodge secretary, the late Brother Adam McNeilly, who was also Worshipful District Master of Ballymoney District LOL16, how I might go about getting O'Hara's True Blues back on the road. He gave me a number of instructions that I conveyed back to my peers in Bendooragh. By now, we had about eight people willing to join and our first task was to persuade five members of the defunct lodge to come back and take the helm for at least a year. So, we visited as many former members as we knew of and soon had the required five.

On the first Wednesday evening in September 1985, the five senior men along with district officers, guests and myself, all met in the partly refurbished Orange Hall under gaslight and the lodge was re-born. It was a proud moment for me, and the following month my friends and helpers were initiated into the lodge. O'Hara's True Blues was truly back in business!

At first inspection, the old banner looked beyond repair. It had been taken good care of during its exile in a clean dry attic but too many wet and windy Twelfths during the fifties and sixties had taken their toll. The stitching was rotten and the surround cloth was stained with old damp. The portrait featuring the late Bro Rev J O'Hara from whom the lodge derived its name was cracked and lined. Buying a new banner was out of the question so careful surgery with an expert hand – or hands – was required! A willing seamstress was found and a painter gave Rev O'Hara a face-lift and the finished product was a banner that would last a few years.

On the evening of 11th July 1986, we who had joined the resurrected lodge did our best to join in the revelry of the traditional village bonfire and singing of Orange songs. However, the next day was to the fore of all our thoughts. Some of us had marched in bands on the Twelfth and I had even walked with my former lodge in 1985 but this year would be different. This year we would be walking with our own lodge, a lodge we had jointly recreated from nothing! As the embers of the bonfire glowed and then dimmed, we sat in the summer night planning our big day over and over again until there was nothing left to say. Wearily, we parted company to get the bare minimum of sleep in preparation for the Twelfth.

I did not need anyone to waken me on the morning of 12th July 1986. I got up with a jump, my stomach in knots with nervous excitement. We were to meet at the hall at 9:00am and it was hard finding something to do during the two hours until then. I donned my suit, collected my much-fingered collarette and walked proudly, yet nervously, to the Orange Hall from my parents' home. At the hall there was a literal buzz of excitement as everyone gathered for the big day. When we unfurled the old banner, we all thought the late Bro Rev J O'Hara never looked better! The banner poles had been sanded and varnished to complement the fresh-faced portrait and the leather straps were given to the banner carriers. After some last minute business, we parted company to make our way to Ballycastle. We did not hire a bus but crammed into cars with my father's roof rack utilised as an ideal courier for the banner poles.

I still remember distinctly coming into the gathering field in Ballycastle. Although it wasn't a very bright day, the sun was making determined efforts to break through a thin cloud and, more often than not, succeeded to bring some sunshine to a momentous occasion. The rattle of Lambeg drums, the rolls of side drums, the tuning of bagpipes and the whistles of flutes mingled with the sound of a hundred accordions as everyone got ready to walk. As we had no band, we had to fall in behind the lodge number next to ours. As the host district left the field, we duly raised the old banner behind our brethren in Dunaghy No Surrender LOL 791 who were led by Dunaghy Accordion Band.

The first steps we took out of the field on to the road were akin to the first steps Neil Armstrong took when he walked on the moon. The realisation that history had been made and that no matter what the future held, something memorable had just happened. I was particularly pleased to hear bystanders comment on how young we all were (that never happens now!) and how it was "a credit to youse". More than a few expressed genuine surprise and delight to see "Bendooragh" back on the road. Because the lodge had folded when we were very young, we maybe didn't realise how many older people would have remembered the former brethren walking behind that same banner. A breeze off the sea caused the banner to flutter and contort and for a while I was afraid that it might undo the work of those who had made it presentable. My worries were unfounded, though, and the pride I felt at being there, wearing the blue collarette with 804 emblazoned thereon, surpassed any fears I may have had about anything that day.

I was not the only one to feel so happy and so elated at walking in a lodge of our own making. The other members felt the same. Although the original five senior men who returned to enable us to resurrect the lodge have all passed away, I remember well their faces that day. I remember thinking, as they waved to people along the route, smiling and shouting hello that they had derived as much from the experience as we had. It struck me that none of the five had ever joined another lodge after the old lodge fell. Maybe their hearts were always in O'Hara's True Blues but circumstances had not allowed them to keep the old lodge going? I never asked them about it; I simply enjoyed watching them as they strode with pride along the route in Ballycastle.

When we got to the field, we carefully laid the banner out on the dry grass. We exchanged a plethora of views and comments on how we each thought it had gone. I know now – and probably knew then – that it was mainly talk for the sake of it. After all, you couldn't go far wrong, walking in a procession from one place to another. Yet that was no mundane chore for us and I suppose we were determined not to let it seem like one. We talked up the walk itself, the quality of the banner and the reception from bystanders. Instead of me telling the others that I had heard five or six people comment about seeing Bendooragh back on the road again, I suggested that I had heard "countless" folk saying it. Our banner was no longer decades old, patched and worn; it was the best banner there and no other banner had a King William as good as ours! The exaggeration we all indulged in was, I suppose, the optimism of youth mingled with the pride and excitement of being a part of what we had achieved.

The walk back from the field after the platform proceedings had concluded was "wee buns" to us. We still felt as proud as before but we were now old hands at it, having completed the main walk earlier that day! I remember thinking that the contrast in ages of our members could not have been sharper. The senior men were all in their sixties and seventies, we had two in their forties and the rest of us were in our teens. Yet on that glorious Twelfth, the senior men stepped out the route as lively as we did. At the end of the parade, we bid good day to the Dunaghy Brethren, thanking them for letting us follow in behind them and headed for Bendooragh. That night, we younger members didn't go anywhere. We simply sat outside the hall and talked about the day we had had and I think it was only then that we realised what we had done. It was not groundbreaking or earth shattering. Yet we realised that as Orangemen, we had achieved much in a short time and our average age was only 18. We went home that night satisfied that we had started something that would succeed and grow – we went home determined that it would.

Today the lodge has 30 members and plays an active role in the community and at as many Orange events as possible. We have adopted a strict dress code and disciplinary code and we now have four Lambeg drums to choose from come the Twelfth. I have enjoyed every Twelfth in the last 21 years and the thrill of walking in the ranks of O'Hara's True Blues has never left me. However, it must be said that 12th July 1986 was – and always will be – a truly glorious Twelfth!

Gary Blair, Ballymoney

The Twelfth in the 1960s

A Twelfth of July day in the early 1960s. My grandfather was Grand Master of the local lodge for 26 years and my dad was also Worshipful Master after that, I had been going to parades since the end of the 2nd World War.

When I became 17 in 1956 my cousin and I joined the local lodge. We were given the qualifications of an Orangeman, to read beforehand on that Twelfth morning we were initiated into the lodge, we got a lecture on what was required of an Orangeman and the standards to be upheld as a member.

I remember in the early 1960s as we walked on the Twelfth morning all the members would turn out in their Sunday best.

To most people the Twelfth was the big day of the year. Everyone was friendly and excited as the weather was nearly always beautiful. I was always very interested in the Lambeg drums and being young with plenty of energy I got plenty of drumming, as a lot of the older people were

Ballynagarrick LOL in 1961

only too glad to let us drum. Back then the crowds at demonstrations were enormous, we still get crowds of over 100,000 at Scarva on a good day on the 13th but that is what the Twelfth was like in the early 1960s. As well as that being just 17 and with the arrival of the 'Mini Skirt' all of a sudden girls seemed a lot more attractive and as you walked in the procession you would catch the eye of a lot of nice girls which made the walk a lot more pleasant. Oh, to be 17 again!

When our lodge came back to Portadown we always paraded the entire town. That was a wonderful experience each year, the crowds were enormous, we would go down what was then called the terminal to Corcrain Orange Hall and it was lined with people, mums, dads, grandfathers, grandmothers and children. Never any trouble, I cannot believe how things got so bad on Garvaghy Road in the late 1990s. I am old but I still walk and stand by the principles of the institution. If everyone did that we would all have a new Ulster to live in, Orange parades should offend no-one and Orangemen should uphold the principles of the Order.

George Wilson, Portadown

The Twelfth of July 2006

THE night before we put up our Ulster flag. Then the next morning (the Twelfth), we left early to get to the parade in Castlederg in time.

We parked in the Castlederg car park and met up there with our granny and grandad Porter in Omagh.

We got our deckchairs and put them down not so far from the entrance and left our grandad while me and my granny went to the stalls.

My two brothers and my dad left us to join up with other people out of their lodge. My sister met a friend and they went off round the stalls together. While we were going round the stalls we came across one with a chocolate fountain. We all got marshmallows on a stick covered in chocolate. There was a lot of chocolate left on the plates so we licked the chocolate off. My mum said we looked like chocolate monsters.

We finally came back to where we had left our grandad and sat down waiting for the parade to start. We could hear some of them tuning up and we could smell the burger, chip and sausage vans.

The parade started. We all looked out for our brothers and dad and when they walked past we all gave them a wave. We all shared a packet of crisps and a bag of raspberry ruffles.

After the first parade we found our brothers and dad and went back to our car for a picnic. After our picnic we walked up the town and then back to our spaces. When our dad walked by when they marched the second time, my wee brother James who was three walked the rest of the way with him. We also met friends from our old church.

After all the marching we went to our Granny Porter's for a lovely tea. In the back seat of our car was a bag with my dad's white gloves, his black marching hat and his collarette and my brothers' collarettes.

That night we went home exhausted, tired but happy.

Grace Porter, Age 11, Markethill

The Bands at the Twelfth

As a wee boy living in Ballyclare, County Antrim, the Twelfth celebrations always held a huge fascination for me. It was the bands, particularly the rhythms of the drums that made the spectacle so outstanding in its own field. Ballyclare is one of those sleepy places with a distinctive Main Street and a town hall so typical of small Ulster towns. It lies in the beautiful Sixmilewater Valley adjacent to many of County Antrim's better known and much larger towns. But Ballyclare did have a march on everywhere else as far as I was concerned, it had a championship flute band: Ballyclare Victoria. I can remember all those years ago seeing the band after they first won a major championship in the Ulster Hall, it would have been 1960, I was all of five years of age. They were magnificent. I decided then that I wanted more than anything else to be a drummer in this band.

So it was only going to me a matter of time before my younger brother and myself joined the ranks of the band. We did that, in fact it was to be in 1966, I was 11 and my kid brother eight. I have been in the band ever since, well except for a period of 12 years when I toured with many dance bands playing drums. However I was to regret leaving the band, even though I was a semi-professional musician earning good money. I missed my mates and the craic of being amongst the ranks of Ballyclare Victoria. My young brother Alan however has been a member without blemish since 1966, that's 41 years. Alan is now an accomplished flautist whereas yours truly still beats the drums. This band of ours in the town of Ballyclare can proudly boast winning the coveted World Championship for Senior Flute bands on no fewer than 23 occasions. Most of the musicians would have made the decision to join after being inspired by watching the band of yesteryear on the street, predictably on the Twelfth when both band and lodge proudly strutted their stuff. In recalling the Twelfth of July of yesteryear, it is that festival that initially sowed the seed of my love and pursuit of music making. Way back in the 60s there was never any mention of offending people, the folk in Ballyclare irrespective of class and creed respected each other, so much so that often our Roman Catholic neighbours were the first on the pavement on those sunny Twelfth mornings as the band and lodge marched down the street to the bus station to be transported to whichever town was hosting the day's celebration. Great days indeed, rich and rare our cultural heritage is, and inclusive too.

Today the Twelfth has still survived, a little battered and bruised perhaps. It is arguably overdue some form of reinvention, but if the merits and distinctions of yesteryear can be included in the new style of the 21st century, living as we do now so harmoniously with one another, then celebrating our cultural heritage in years to come should be quite exciting. Potentially we are all winners whether Protestant, Catholic or dissenter. We have so much in common in sharing this piece of real estate, therefore celebrating each other's heritage is of paramount importance. We were able to engage as friends irrespective of our cultural differences in the 60s on the Twelfth in this lovely part of County Antrim.

So we can do so again with renewed vigour. Down through the years this band has marched throughout County Antrim, and our audience was always at its peak and most appreciative on the Twelfth Day. The welcome and hard earned applause of the spectators lining the route always ensured that the adrenalin flowed through the veins of the musicians. The craic in the band was mighty, and everybody got a rub now and again, there was not one of us escaped being the butt of many's a joke. For a long time we had a mascot who sadly is no longer with us. I refer to the late, great Maurice Watt. Maurice suffered from Down's Syndrome, I say suffered but that is not true, his world was a magical place. He was truly a great character who followed our fortunes for many many years. He was officially a member. Now every Twelfth when we got back to Ballyclare in the evening Maurice was tasked with leading the band around the town. That was the highlight of his day. The people in the town would give him special encouragement as he proudly lead from the front, his chest swelled to enormous proportions with a big smile on his face.

Often the band played innocent tricks on Maurice, but he was cute and often got the better of the band on more than one occasion. The one trick he always fell for was the sidestep. Upon approach to the hall and only to the drumbeat marking time the band were right behind him but at an appointed time the band would quietly swing and walk in another direction leaving Maurice on his own. Boy did he get mad, then the big smile would return and everything would be back to normal. Moments like this were precious but sadly Maurice passed on. We still have fond memories of the wee man and always will have. He was famous throughout banding. When we played at the Ulster Hall in competition Maurice sat on the platform quietly playing with his trademark ball of string which continually was fed and twisted through his nimble fingers. But the Twelfth was Maurice's big day, and he was always turned out like a new pin, the knot on his tie was his pride and joy.

Many times throughout the day or at the field the tie was checked and re-checked.

For too long it has been allowed to go unchecked that the Twelfth celebrations are sectarian, they are not. But in fairness some discipline may be required to properly regulate the festival, this is a must. In looking back and remembering with fondness how it used to be, that is a wonderful template for future generations to use in order to make the festival truly all-inclusive and such a spectacle. Maurice was our beacon of hope, he kept us all sane and we cherish his memory. He never new how to hate, never focused on anything without his smile, that made us all smile especially on the Twelfth.

Ian Moore, Ballymena

The Twelfth 1945

The Second World War was over and I was a 14 year old lad who was looking forward to attending the first Twelfth parade since before the outbreak of war. It had been a 'hive of activity' on the farm for the last few weeks. All the hedges had been cut, the gates were painted, the outhouses were given a coat of white-wash and everything was looking its best for the Twelfth.

Inside the house, there was much activity and the smell of baking and cooking wafted from the kitchen.

The Orange Hall, both inside and outside, was tidied up, and each night in the week leading up to the Twelfth my father and myself would go to the hall and help the others who had come to prepare the Lambeg drums.

"You will have to wear your suit" my mother said, and this I have done on every Twelfth since then. On the eleventh night my mother had made sure that all the shoes were polished and placed in rows for my brothers and myself. My sisters had new clothes for the Twelfth and these would be worn as Sunday best for the rest of the year.

I woke up early on the Twelfth morning, hoping to see the sun shining through my window, if it was raining, it would mean that the Lambeg drums would have to be left at home. It would also mean that I would not be needed for a very important role in the Twelfth Parade.

The farm duties were done quickly, and the countryside was quiet. It was just like a Sunday morning, except for the sound of one or two Lambeg drums which could be heard in the distance and whose beat carried over the countryside.

I was eager to get to the Orange Hall in case I was needed for my very important role. On previous Twelfths I had always wanted to be first to get to the Orange Hall so that I would be sure to get a Junior Collarette. There were always more children than collarettes so someone was disappointed. Usually this disappointment was forgotten when a boy or girl was given the job of carrying the strings of the banner. I was too old for that now. I had a much more important role to perform, so I was happy to leave those jobs to the younger boys in their short trousers.

I had been asked to carry the repair kit for the Lambeg drums. This kit was in a small metal box with a hinged lid. In it were a number of very thin pieces of dried goatskin and special glue to stick on the patches. I had spent many hours split-ting the dried goatskin to make the finest (thinnest) 'patches'. This kit would be needed to make emergency repairs if a drumhead began to crack or break.

With my metal box in my pocket, I joined the drummers at the front of the parade from the Orange Hall. The banner fluttered in the light breeze. The vibrant orange of the Orange lilies and the reds and whites of the sweet William which adorned the banner poles were joined this year by black ribbons tied on each side of the banner in memory of those from the lodge who had been killed in the War.

The boys holding the strings were given instructions on how slow or fast to walk in order to keep the banner upright. I looked around from my position at the front of the parade and saw lines of men, each in their Orange regalia, and dressed in their Sunday best suits, walking to the beat of the Lambeg drums.

The cattle grazing in the nearby fields first came to the hedge to see what was happening, then thundered away tails in the air when the Lambeg drums drew near.

I walked along the road with a sense of great pride alongside neighbours and friends, with the thunder of the Lambegs in my ears. I was following in my father's footsteps and hoping that he would be proud of me and that I would be able to play a part in the parade.

If a drum head didn't develop a hole then maybe I would be asked to carry a drummer's coat as different people took turns at drumming the Lambegs.

We made our way to the Maze Station (sadly this station closed many years ago) where we boarded the train for Lisburn. The sun was shining and the sky was clear, I was happy as I knew that the drummers were going to be able to drum the Lambeg drums to the field.

Huge crowds lined the streets of Lisburn, I had never seen so many people in one place before, and everyone seemed to be happy and laughing. The streets were adorned with line upon line of Union Jacks, and there was an air of excitement around every corner. On and on we walked through the streets our feet marching to the beat of the drums, then I heard my name being called, a drum had developed a hole, and I was needed. A repair would have to be done before the drum head would split, or burst like a balloon.

The drummer with the ailing Lambeg drum and I stepped out of the parade and eased our way through the crowd and found a quiet spot to try and do repairs. Out came the metal box from my pocket and the repairs began, not one but two patches were needed. With trembling fingers I found patches that would be the right size for the holes that were beginning to appear in the drum head. The glue was applied and the patches stuck on, within minutes we rejoined our lodge and I slipped the metal box back into my suit pocket, ready if it were needed again.

We marched on towards the field at Strawberry Hill, Ballynahinch Road, Lisburn and I was hoping that my uncle would be there. He would give me half a crown, he always did on the Twelfth, but this year I would surely have earned it, I would tell him about my very important role and maybe show him the patches on the drum.

It seemed like no time at all until the arch at the field entrance came into view and I read the word Welcome on it, I knew that the other side of the arch read Safe Home and I wondered if this applied to people and Lambeg drums or would my services be needed on the homeward journey.

I followed the drummers to where they rested their drums and joined them as the tea and ham sandwiches were handed out. The men talked about the drums and about how they were drumming and about the problem with the drum head. I was praised for my help with the repairs.

Some time later I went to find my father and mother, as I wanted to tell them about my part in the drum repair. I also knew that my mother would have with her a tin box which contained some special treats. Would it be wheaten bread with roast beef, or would it be buns or cake? There had been smells of cooking and baking around the house for days, but there had been no cakes or buns on the tea table.

The War and rationing had made it difficult to get even the most basic of ingredients, so buns and cakes were a very special treat indeed.

My mother had brought roast beef and wheaten bread, buns and fruit bread and I ate everything that I was offered. It seemed to taste much better in the field. My father greeted his brother-in-law with a hearty handshake and after some banter about getting tall and Lambeg drums I was given the much awaited half a crown. Now I was rich, and I took my time in choosing what I wanted to buy.

Even though I went through the motions of looking at every stall very carefully, holding my half a crown tightly in my hand, I knew that I would eventually choose to spend some or maybe all of it on ice cream. How wonderful it tasted, as it cooled my mouth on this hot summer day, and I licked each melting drop so that none was wasted. There hadn't been any ice cream in the War years, so how wonderful it was to taste its cool sweetness. The time passed quickly as I talked to the other boys that I knew from school. I told them of my role and how I had helped to repair the drum. I even showed some of them the drum and its patches. On the platform the guest speaker was making his speech and most of the older men were standing around listening to what was being said. After a while there was the sound of applause and the speeches were over.

Soon I heard the sound of a number of Lambeg drums playing in unison. This was it, this was the time when the drummers from all the lodges formed a circle and had a "tune". There were twelve or fourteen drums in the circle when I pushed my way through the spectators who had gathered to enjoy the drum music.

I stood beside my lodge drums, watching for any holes that might appear.

"Do you want a tune young fella?" I was asked, but I shook my head and moved away a step or two. Soon it was time to parade home. I checked my pocket to make sure that I had the box; I was ready if I was needed.

The parade headed home from the field through Lisburn, the crowds had now gone but a few people still stood at the street corners. We boarded the train with our Lambegs still intact and our patches still holding firm.

I helped with the 'slacking out' of the drums in the Orange Hall, this is where the drum heads are loosened and taken out of the drums. The drums were stored with their painting or picture facing outwards ready for the following year.

I walked the short distance home with my younger brothers and sisters who were allowed to walk with my father and I on the last part of the parade home.

The routine of farm life began again as I changed out of my suit. The tin box was taken out of my suit pocket and placed on the table beside my bed. The patches that were used from the box would need to be replaced, and that I would do as soon as possible.

That Twelfth of July 1945 was a day that has stuck in my mind as the day when I realised I had a role to play in the Orange Order. Over the years that have followed I have had many roles within the Order, and each Twelfth awakens the same excitement and sense of pride in me, as it did in 1945 as I walk dressed in my suit and orange collarette with my fellow brethren to the wonderful beat of the Lambeg drum.

Irene Montgomery, Lisburn (Written on behalf of a 76 year old relative)

The Burning of
the Shankill Road Arch

MY memories of the Twelfth go back to when I was a boy in the 50s and the event of the burning of the Orange Arch in one of the streets of the Shankill called Pernau Street, which was off Berlin Street.

Like all stories it has a beginning but in this case it had a tragic ending for all concerned.

Like most children I was brought up in one of those two-up-two-down houses, what were then called Corporation homes that mushroomed all around the Shankill Road. At least it did have a toilet even if it was outside, nothing to really write home about, when it rained the water came flooding through what we called the back yard and soaked everything that it touched.

This was a street where most of the men worked in the shipyard, including my father and grandfather who, by the way, was one of the thousands of men who worked on the ill-fated Titanic.

Most of the mothers in the street worked the 6pm-10pm shift in Ewarts Mill, the street turned black with mothers going to the mill to earn a few shillings to bring home and help feed their families.

What I remember about my own mother is when she came home I would get a large kettle of boiling hot water and wash her tired and sore feet. Like other mothers she worked in her bare feet standing on a duck board in the mill for four hours.

My mother had to give up her job because there was a baby on the way. I remember the day when that child, a little girl was born. As a young boy I could hear all the fuss going on in the bedroom and I asked if there was anything that I could do to help my mother, such was the innocence of a child.

The birth of the child brought joy into a home that had very little to celebrate, there were no holidays ever, the only big event in the year was the Sunday School trip organised by the local Methodist Church to the seaside at Ballywalter.

The other great event that was going to happen this year and was different was that for the first time, Pernau Street was going to put up an Orange Arch. This was new for the street. A few streets away Brussels Street had an Orange Arch and then there was the famous Orange Arch of Malvern Street which really was a sight to behold.

For Pernau Street this was the year to top all years. We had a new Queen who was just crowned and then as children we all had a pencil case which we received at school with a bar of chocolate in it, along with a coronation mug with a portrait of our new Queen on the side. Then there was a wonderful street party and we could eat as much as we wanted.

It seemed that all year the street had prepared for this great event when we would have our own arch. The men were busy with their hammers and saws, the women sewing red, white and blue flowers. The bunting was in abundance, the silver and golden stars shone like the real thing glittering in the sunlight.

From flag poles it was the Union Jacks as we had no Ulster flags then. There were streamers everywhere from house to house. The footpath was painted in the colours red, white and blue to show our devoted loyalty to our new Queen.

As children it seemed that the only job we could do was collect bonfire wood or steal it from the gang in the next street. That is until they wised up to what was happening with their own wood, then they stationed guards who were looking for an enemy in the night.

In getting up to those antics we never dreamed that not only would we have our own bonfire of the sleepers and the usual chairs and settee that grace a bonfire, but also our own arch that was made all year round and was put up in the middle of a time of great celebration.

There was not one person present then, who would ever have thought that this arch was going to be torn down and burned by the street that with loving hands made it. There was not one person present then that imagined that this arch was going to be the focal point of deep mourning.

The Orange day was going to be a black day, many tears were going to be wept in that street, when one of the children that danced under that arch was going to be carried in a coffin down that street and by the two homes that supported that arch.

This child was my sister, a young child of four-years-of-age. As my father was painting the railings in front of our wee house with bright red paint for the 12th of July celebrations, I looked up and saw my sister on fire from head to foot.

I said "Dad look at Evelyn!" At that moment I could see my dad kicking the bright red paint out of the way. That paint for a long time stained the ground just outside our home like a mural or memorial to my sister.

As I looked up the street Mrs Henderson had blankets which she pulled off the bed and she was wrapping my precious sister in them. The milkman had a canvas sheet which he had taken of his milk float and he was trying to extinguish the flames.

Unknown to us at the time my younger sister Evelyn had taken a box of matches out of the house. These matches belonged to my grandfather who was a pipe smoker.

Children as we know have a fascination with fire. To her peril my sister was striking match after match and somehow her dress caught fire and she was enveloped in flames as a living inferno that seemed to light up the street.

At once she was rushed to the Royal Victoria Hospital for Sick Children. She lay in one ward and my father lay in the next ward and from his body the doctors took layer upon layer of skin to try and save her life but it was a battle that they sadly lost and she died. The news of her death spread from street to street and there was an outpouring of grief that one would have thought our new Queen had passed away.

The support that we received as a devastated family from that wee street was amazing, the love shown to me and thoughtfulness has remained with me for 54 years.

The thing that compounded the pain was that she died on my mother's birthday a few days after the 12th of July. The thing that my mother treasured like a rare and precious diamond was a wee pair of cheap trainers that my sister wore when she was burnt. Those trainers were kept in a cardboard box in the wardrobe until both my mother and father died within a year and ten months of each other and then I disposed of them.

The other thing that compounded the pain was that my father was not allowed to go to his four-year-old daughter's funeral. On the day of the funeral he was still in hospital, and on that sad day the nurse wheeled him in his wheelchair onto a balcony and he looked down on the coffin of his wee girl that he could not carry. Only God knows the broken heart that he had at that time.

The whole of Pernau Street was in deep mourning because that street had lost one of its own, there was not one adult that had a heart for any 12th of July celebrations or Orange Arch. At once a decision was taken that the arch would be pulled down and destroyed.

Even now I can hear the very people who worked all year to create this wonderful arch deciding that it must be destroyed. This was spoken of very openly on the street at the time and everyone was in agreement as to what must be done.

From that 12th of July in 1953 there has never been an Orange Arch in Pernau Street off the Shankill Road, it was the day that the dream of having an Orange arch died.

This was the first and this was the last Orange Arch for many years. The death of that child seemed to haunt that very street as children were warned as they grew up never to play with matches.

Within our home for years the Twelfth was not a time of rejoicing, but a time of mourning and deep sadness and much crying.

After that event as you can imagine my mother was never the same again, for years she suffered greatly in her mind. The other thing is that the whole event manifested itself in having a smothering effect on me as the eldest child and when at the age of 11 the doctor thought that I was going to die, her reaction was to run screaming out of the room repeating that she could not face losing another child.

To both my parents' delight after a prolonged time in hospital I pulled through and their worst nightmare was over.

The events of that Twelfth were never forgotten in our home. The way that my dad seemed to deal with his grief was in the drink which seemed to intensify during the Twelfth holidays. It was his way of escape. Even now I can see him with his head bowed and repeating Evelyn's name again and again, and when my first child was born, he took her in his arms and said: "God has given me my Evelyn back." Yes he said it in drink, but to him it was a reality.

My sister was too young to recall that awful Twelfth .

I had to receive counselling from a child psychologist because every time I read in my school reader anything about fire I would panic as I recalled seeing my sister as a ball of fire that terrible Twelfth.

For years seeing a bonfire brought back awful memories of 1953 when we thought that it was a year to really celebrate.

The Orange Arch was pulled down and burnt because tragedy hit Pernau Street off the Shankill that 12th of July in 1953. That street and the Armour family would never be the same again, how could it be?

James Armour, Belfast

My Memories of the Twelfth

I was born in Nurse Linton's Nursing Home in Whitehead on the 12th July 1938 as a band was leading the local lodge to the railway station on the first stage of their journey to the field.

Mum thought she was having a boy, to be called John after my grandfather. When she had a girl her first words were "What am I going to call her," and the answer from Dr. Grey, a canny man, was "You could always call her Dolly but I haven't heard her braying yet".

How could I not love the Twelfth after a start like that - the bands, the banners and especially the Lambeg drums. I thought they were all just for my birthday - my very own birthday party.

Of course, after a few years I found out that they were not really for me - but what the heck, as far as I was concerned it was always going to be for my birthday - I just loved it. I still love the bands, the banners and of course, my favourite the Lambeg drums. I now have a CD of the Lambeg so that I can listen to them all year round.

I am now getting on a bit and will be 70 on the Twelfth this year. Who knows, maybe it will soon be a case of sitting at home and watching my birthday party on TV. But what a birthday party - you could not beat it and here is to many more of them.

Joan McClelland, Portrush

County Fermanagh Orange Celebrations held at Lisnakea
- 12th July 2003

The following is a report on the 12th July seen through the eyes of an exiled Lisnaskea man

The procession took place from the marshalling field at Derryree to the 'speech' field at Cushwash, a distance of approx two miles (basically straight through the town along Main Street).

At the front were four period dressed infantrymen of Col.Tiffany's Regiment, later to become the 27th Regt. of Foot, which became the Royal Inniskilling Fusiliers. They escorted 'King William' riding a white horse. Then came the Officers of the Fermanagh Grand Lodge, plus a visitor namely DGM Northern Province of England - John Armstrong, led by the CGM Roy Kells.

An impressive array of Orangemen and women followed, walking proudly behind their bands and their banners.

Lodges from the counties of Monaghan, Cavan, Leitrim and Donegal came directly after the Grand Lodge and they did their counties and Orangeisim proud, very proud indeed.

This year, there seemed to be far more 'quality' bands than in previous years, including silver bands, parts-playing flute bands and many stately pipe bands. I especially enjoyed the silver parts-playing flute bands - I wonder if they have a tape out (there were two of these bands) as I certainly would be in the market for one or two.

The weather was perhaps more suited to watching rather than marching, being rather warm, and, certainly, the older brethren were grateful to have it dry enough to sit on the grass and rest tired legs, whilst listening to the speeches at the field. These were very interesting and non political but another medical emergency meant proceedings had to be cut short. Sadly, there had already been a fatality on the walk among the Rosslea Brethren.

The Fermanagh Twelfth was indeed a terrific family day. Everyone, especially the children, really enjoyed themselves. I saw no bad behaviour or unpleasantness, only thousands of happy people greeting old friends and enjoying their traditional demonstration day in a most relaxed manner. (As I remember, that's the way it has always been)

Well done Fermanagh!

Bro. John Armstrong, Lisnaskea

LOL No 1300

Aged 3 in the Field at Finaghy on 12th July 1952

We lived at Mountcollyer Avenue, off North Queen Street, in North Belfast. At the time L.O.L 1300 was the largest Orange Lodge in Ireland with some 200 brethren. My uncle John and grandfather, who did a bit of degree work, were also in the Lodge.

That morning I remember especially the lodge members and Shaftsbury Pipe Band gathered outside 62 Mountcollyer Avenue. Our house was packed to overflowing with men eating sandwiches and drinking tea. Then this man walked in wearing his kilt, tunic and this enormous bearskin. I was absolutely terrified and ran screaming to my mum, I had never seen a Kilty before. Actually I did quite well out of that experience. The Orangemen and bandsmen all took pity on me and had a whip round.

The band and lodge members including my older brother Billy and cousin Jim assembled in the avenue. Before moving off the band played Psalm 23 and the Green Grassy Slopes of the Boyne with the lodge members and everyone in the avenue joining in. This was tradition 1300 had for many years. They then moved off to tremendous cheers from the residents of the avenue, it was a lovely day. The Orangemen in their bowler hats, white gloves and dark grey suit, their collarettes were tailor made and were quite unique. They appeared to be made of silk.

My mum and the rest of us headed for the field by train, and watched the parade at the bridge on Finaghy Road North. As Sandy Row approached a big cheer went up from my mum and aunts. When the Rising Sons of India arrived I was taken into the ranks by my dad and was dressed in his collar and bowler. When we arrived in the field we always seemed to be under the same tree. We had tea and sandwiches, everyone seemed to be happy even when they stood in cow pat, which there seemed to be plenty of.

When the men arrived back in the avenue they had a tremendous reception from the people from all round the North Queen Street. Before breaking ranks the band played another hymn followed by the Sash, then the National Anthem, everyone seemed to sing with gusto. The men were then treated to refreshments at no 62. A great day was had by all.

The Rising Sons of India, Loyal Orange Lodge 1300 Sandy Row District was founded during the Indian Mutiny by Irish Soldiers.

During the Indian Campaign the lodge secretary was a warrant officer who was shot in the chest. He carried the lodge warrant in his breast pocket and it was splattered with his blood. The lodge then became known as the lodge with the blood-stained warrant. As far as I am aware the soldier did not die as a result of his wound.

John Kennedy, Newtownabbey

The Twelfth

My childhood memories of the Twelfth began when I was four or five, around 1967-1968. My father Thomas was an Orangeman in a local lodge and carried the banner every Twelfth along with another man Stanley Hillis. The lodge was Carrickawilken and it had a flute band, both mostly consisting of my mother's relations. I carried the strings of the banner.

It all began early on the Twelfth morning. My mother would have given us a hearty breakfast. My father wore his suit and my three older brothers played in the band, one the triangle, one the cymbals and the other the drum. They wore white shirts, red ties and black trousers with matching caps. Because my father did not drive we all walked out two long lanes, past Catholic homes to the main road to be lifted by the Worshipful Master of the lodge, Willie Adams in his Morris Minor. We were taken to the Orange hall right on the border's edge located on the Mountainy Road, now Clay Road. The band played down the road a bit, accompanied by the banner and Orangemen, to well wishers before proceeding by bus to the town where the Twelfth was being held.

Carrying the strings of the banner filled me with pride those days long ago walking near to my father. I held those strings tightly and was tired after my day walking. On return to the hall in the evening, I recall the very hot tea, the thick sandwiches and the big buns. I also remember a Catholic man from the town providing us with orange linen to decorate the big drum of the band.

Kenneth Gordon, Keady

Twelfth Memories

Everyone thinks the Twelfth is all about Orangemen and Orangewomen and don't forget the bandsmen. I write this story as a person from behind the scenes.

I am the wife of an Orangeman, I am not complaining, I love every minute of it and this is what the Twelfth of July means to me and to my four friends who are also the wives of Orangemen, all from the same Lodge which is LOL55 Raloo True Blues.

We are unofficially LOL55 Ladies Section, and we see the Twelfth as an opportunity to fund raise for our husbands' beloved lodge. We sell tea, sandwiches, buns etc. in the field.

Our planning begins the week before the Twelfth and boy what decisions do we have to make, how many teabags do we need? How much milk do we need? Who will get these? Who is making buns? Who is making tray bakes? Who is doing the egg and onion? Who is doing the tuna and onion? All the time wondering to ourselves why did we say we would do this again this year. Could we not just have a break this year and just watch the parade like everybody else, but truth be told although it is hard work, it is such good fun we all have a laugh and enjoy the company on the day and we wouldn't have it any other way.

Then the hard work begins, on 10th July on go the aprons, out come the baking bowls. The day is spent weighing out flour, beating eggs, making up the mixture for those lovely buns that go down so well with a refreshing cup of tea after that long walk.

After a day spent slaving in the kitchen comes the satisfaction of seeing all that hard work transformed into dozens and dozens of lovely buns and tray bakes. The next stage is fighting off the hungry hands who want to start eating these already, but they cannot be touched until the Twelfth.

Then comes the 11th July and the next stage in the planning is a trip to the shops first thing in the morning. With 30 loaves neatly stacked in the shopping trolley and ignoring all the funny looks we proceed to the checkout eager to get back home as there is such a lot to be done. Home then to boil dozens of eggs, painfully chop lots of onions, mash tuna, wash lettuce, chop chicken, butter hundreds of slices of bread, make the sandwiches all up, put them into plastic sandwich trays, label them and finally store them in the fridges overnight. Who says housewives don't get RSI. The kitchen is then all tidied up but that smell of egg and onion will linger for days.

Then comes the big day itself and it's off to an early start, with the trailer all nicely scrubbed up and loaded with gazebo, water, cooker, tables, chairs teapots and of course buns and sandwiches off we go hoping to get a good spot in the field.

We get set up long before the parade even sets off. This is when we get a chance to relax and have a chat, usually over breakfast. Then we get a dander around the other stalls. We resist the urge to buy the funny hats and red, white and blue wigs.

A couple of hours later we hear the sound of bands heading our way. The rush is on then to get the water boiled up and the teapots ready in anticipation of the big rush from the tired and hungry marchers who will want a seat, cup of tea, something to eat and somewhere to take their shoes off and rest a while.

The day just flies in. We have the satisfaction of seeing the same faces coming to our stall who were there last year, at least we know we have a good reputation at our stall. Then after a final rush before the parade forms up again for the return journey we get the stall packed up. It is our turn now to watch the parade so we stand for nearly two hours on already weary feet enjoying the spectacle of the Orangemen and bands on the return march.

Time now to go home with the beat of the drums still ringing in our ears and the smell of egg and onion still lingering in the house, but with the satisfaction of knowing that we have raised enough money to help keep our beloved wee lodge solvent for another while.

It has been hard work and time consuming, but it has also been a great day out. We love doing it and couldn't imagine spending the Twelfth Day any other way. What a surprise it was to see our photograph, which was taken at a previous Twelfth, appear in a leaflet produced by the Orange Order and destined for an exhibition in Washington Mall in America. It makes us proud to be part of the Orange Culture and Orange Family.

Elizabeth Swann, Larne

The Twelfth - A Great Day

It was the 11th night and a warm summer's evening. Final preparations were underway for the big day. The grass was mown, Orange Lillies and Sweet William vying with each other for room in the borders and all was trimmed with box-like hedges. The Snowcem had been mixed and the kerbs which led down to the newly painted gate had been whitened. The customary new brush shaft had been bought and, with the Union Jack firmly tacked on, it had been proudly erected on the front of the house.

The still evening air was broken with the beat of the Lambeg drums and despite the heat smoke curled out of the chimneys of the eight cottages. A fire burnt bright inside to provide the hot water for us seven kids, mum and dad to bathe, although I can't quite recall the bath being emptied nine times. I'm sure we must have shared the bath water.

New clothes were laid out for each of us but pride of place went to dad's clothes. He worked very hard and didn't get much for himself but one thing I always remember was that he had a new white shirt. After what seemed like a hundred pins were taken out it was ironed and hung up along with his newly cleaned suit. His sash was always hung over the picture in the living room with the smaller ones for the boys beside it.

The brass ends of the banner and committee poles were polished by many helping hands. Us children felt that somehow this was a special privilege that we had been given and so felt very important.

The excitement was mounting and none of us were sure how we could sleep because tomorrow would mean wearing our new clothes, and the most thrilling of all it was the 12th of July.

"Get up children, it's the Twelfth," was my dad's alarm call for as long as I remember, but he needn't have bothered as it was the only morning we didn't need called. Dad left early for Marlacoo Orange Hall where he was a proud and faithful member for 50 years. My oldest brother went with him hoping to get a job carrying the strings.

The rest of us waited at home and watched and listened for any sound or sight of the pipe band which would tell us the lodges were on the move. Marlacoo along with their neighbouring brethren Tannaghmore walk from their respective halls, meet up at the top of the Lough Hill and walk about a mile to board the buses to meet the rest of the district in Tandragee.

Finally they appeared, just the same as every year but it was as if you were seeing it for the first time.

The banner blew faintly in the summer wind, the smell of the kilts, the men all smartly dressed and the lilt of the pipes always made this a wonderful spectacle.

It was at this point that we finally got to take part as we joined dad here and

Marlacoo LOL 306 about 35 years ago.
Dad is seated front right

walked very proudly the last few hundred yards to the bus, sometimes being lucky enough to get a banner string.

There was no health and safety regulations then as the bus was packed like sardines with no less than four to a seat but this was all part of the great adventure that the Twelfth was to us children.

The district parade in Tandragee was, in many ways, the best part of the day for it was here that we met many friends that you maybe only saw once a year, and our Uncle Willie always gave us money. We watched in awe as all the lodges formed a unique ring at the top of the town where the National Anthem was played.

We got on the buses again to the main demonstration where we got a good vantage point and had a well-earned rest while we watched the rest of the parade.

Up and away again, this time to 'the field'. We met with dad at 'Ahorey Presbyterian Tent' where we all filed in and sat on planks of wood which rested on apple boxes. The grass beneath your feet was always wet probably because the people threw the dregs of tea out on it, but despite all this we thought we were in a five star hotel as we sat with our wee paper bag complete with ham sandwiches and a wee plain bun.

We again made our way back to watch the homeward parade but when Marlacoo came along we had to follow for the bus. Sometimes we had to walk quite a few miles and I suppose it wasn't but I always remember the Twelfth as warm and hot. It was with some relief and probably more so for mum when we saw the buses.

Waiting back at the hall were the ladies who had made the Twelfth tea. Mrs McClelland was the lady in charge of this particular task for many years and who managed to serve up a delicious tea with very few catering facilities.

The children always played outside until the men had eaten. We were then ushered in to what seemed like a very big hall (which in fact was very small), two big long tables with snow white covers with vases of Orange Lillies and Sweet William adding some colour.

Plates of soda bread, wheaten and sliced loaf lined the middles of the table. Big round plates of beef, gravy and onions were placed in front of us which we ate with great relish (but wouldn't touch at home). We got our own small mineral complete with a straw which was the icing on the cake.

It was a very tired but happy family that made it's way home down the same road the lodge had come that morning.

Dad always said to mum, "You know! That was a great day," and do you know it always was.

Lorraine Hazley, Richhill

What the Twelfth meant to me

AT 6am on the Twelfth morning, it was my turn to milk the cows. I had only been in bed five hours as it was after midnight before we left the Church Hall. I belonged to Richhill Presbyterian Church and we catered for the Orangemen on the Twelfth. On the 11th night we started at 6pm to make sandwiches. In the kitchen the local butcher sliced all the tinned ham with his large slicing machine and no-one was allowed to go near him. A long production line of tables was set up down the hall. At one end, ladies and gentlemen including the minister buttered the bread (600 loaves in total). This was then passed to a group of people who put the ham in and stacked the sandwiches ready for cutting. At the other end of the table two ladies with large knives cut the sandwiches in sets of three and then I was one of the teenagers who wrapped them in grease-proof paper and put them into a white paper bag ready for packing into the large wicker hampers. After all the sandwiches were carefully packed into the hampers, the lorry was loaded with food, tables, chairs, kettles and all the other necessary items for the next day.

So on the Twelfth morning, my whole family had to be at the demonstration field before the roads closed at 8am with 10 gallon creamery cans of fresh milk. Once at the demonstration field it was all action stations. Some of the men lit the coal fires and set the large water boilers on top. It was their job to make sure that as soon as the procession came into the field there would be an everlasting supply of boiling water to make tea. Four elderly ladies set up their station and washed all the cups ready for the day, and they washed cups all day until the food ran out. A band of ladies and children opened all the bags of sandwiches, which were packed last night and added a bun to each bag. Men and boys set all the folding chairs in rows inside the tent where the men sat to take their tea. Two ladies, renowned for their tea-making skills, washed the kettles and prepared them for

My frist Twelfth at the tent

Mrs Brooks manning the boiler, 13th July 1983

making gallons of tea. When all this was done, we were ready for our first cup of tea.

As a young teenager, I looked after the crisp and mineral stall at the front of the tent, and it was here that you had a chance to see many of your school pals and friends. But the best job of all had to be the cashier at the door of the tent. It was here that you met all kinds of people and made many friends and acquaintances who came back year after year. Young Orangemen who were after a date, husbands and wives with small children who didn't know whether they wanted sandwiches or crisps and the older generation who were just glad to get a packed lunch and a good cup of tea.

At the back of the tent where the water was boiled and the kettles of tea made, there were many requests. Mothers asking for a jug of hot water to warm a child's bottle, or the use of a cattle trailer which had brought equipment to the tent, to change a child's nappy in privacy. Many Orangemen left their bowler hats and collarettes in cars so that they wouldn't lose them until the going out procession.

This may all sound like a day's hard work and I admit you were always busy but it didn't seem like work because everyone, the youngest child, to the most senior citizen who would have been in their eighties were working together as a team. Of course, it goes without saying there was a lot of 'craic' among everyone and with members of other organisations also catering on the day. Water, whether cold or boiling, milk and even coal were often exchanged if someone else ran out before they had all their food sold. Orangemen, traditionally went for their tea to their local church or organisation that was catering but if an Orangeman was seen at a rival tent he was in for some banter by his local people and they may even have taken him over a cup of 'good tea' just to keep the craic going.

When all the food was sold, it was time to pack up and this was no mean task. All the chairs and tables had to be folded and carried onto the lorry. All the kettles and utensils had to be washed and carefully packed up again and then it was time to take the tent down. The men usually did this but it wasn't unknown to see a lady or child holding on to a rope as the roof of the tent was lowered to the ground. My greatest pride at this stage was seeing the 'RICHHILL PRESBYTERIAN CHURCH' banner being taken off the top of tent poles, because I made that banner. My mum washed 'flour bags' and I sewed them together and painted the name on them when I was only 14-years-of-age.

After all this was done some of the elderly ladies would have gone for a walk up the field and brought back ice-creams for everyone. What better way could you end a great day?

Unfortunately, in the mid-1990s, due to the uncertainty of which town the Twelfth would be held in, the church gave up their catering activities and the Twelfth has never had the same meaning.

Margaret Black, Richhill

An Orange and Purple Twelfth

I HAVE many memories of Twelfths I attended over the years in different parts of Northern Ireland but the ones from my childhood are most vivid in my memory.

I can still recall the excitement that started several days prior to the big occasion. Hedges were cut and trimmed along the laneside and the grass verges tidied. Inside our farmhouse my mother was as busy as a bee. The windows were stripped of their net curtains and looked naked until redressed by the nets which were then dazzling white having undergone the blue bag treatment. Shirts ballooned on the clothes line like kites and were then brought in and ironed with care. With just the right dampness and the correct heat the box-iron glided over the shirts. I remember watching my mother change the irons in the box. The glowing iron was retrieved from the coals in the big black-leaded range with tongs and inserted in the trap door of the box iron and the cold iron dropped back into the range for the next change over. The kitchen smelt of the warm damp air as the steam rose from the ironing board.

My father's and brothers' suits were brushed and pressed and a clean hankie put in each suit pocket, shoes were polished and clean socks at the ready.

The big brown paper bag, tied at the opening with flour-bag string, was retrieved from the top shelf of the wardrobe. This had been the resting place of my father's hard hat since the previous Twelfth. It was brushed and aired and given a final brush to ensure the pile was all going in the same direction. The sash had been folded away in tissue paper and had the same musty smell as the hard hat. It was also hung out on a hanger to air and to let the creases fall out. We children were washed and scrubbed the night before and my hair rinsed until it was squeaky clean.

The preparations built up an expectant air of excitement on the same par as waiting for the Sunday school excursion or the Church Soiree or even Santa's arrival.

My family belonged to the local Gloonan Lodge No 504, which is one of six lodges that form Ahoghill District. Ahoghill together with the districts of Cullybackey and Portglenone form a triangle for the demonstration and the venue is chosen by rotation and the home lodge or district is designated as the host.

On this particular occasion, which must have been in the early 1940s, the Twelfth was held in Ahoghill. When the last of the milking was done and the livestock fed we all had breakfast around the big kitchen table and the conversation centred on the fact that my two elder brothers were to carry the banner tapes for the first time. They were quite pleased with themselves. My mother reminded the boys to wear their school shoes. "Those Sunday school shoes aren't broken in yet and would cut the heels off you as it's a long walk." The conversation moved to other matters concerning the event - the names of new members of the lodge to those who wouldn't be able to walk the distance and would probably travel by car.

Then it was time to get dressed. My father and two elder brothers prepared first. My mother bustled around giving a final brush to the suit collars. The silver fringe of the sash glinted and jiggled as my mother rolled it carefully and curled it inside the hard hat and handed it to my father.

The lodges file past

"We'll see you in the Field," and then they were off early to get to the Orange Hall in good time.

My mother, youngest brother and I then got ready. I could barely wait to put on my new ankle socks with the pink stripes around the turndowns and to buckle the new brown sandals. The sandals had cream spongy soles and to this day I can still sense their distinctive smell. To crown it all my uncle Bob had given me money to buy a new hair ribbon. At school most of us girls wore our hair parted on the right and the rest combed over to the left where a tuft of hair was tied in a big bow with coloured ribbon. I was constantly losing my ribbons so I was thrilled to get a new pink ribbon to match my ankle socks.

The music could be heard in the distance as we walked up to Ahoghill village. The crowds were beginning to line the streets so mother selected a good spot where we could view the parade. She chatted with neighbours and relatives and even in the fervour of the day they had time to talk about clocking hens and a 'setten' of eggs. My brother and I stood around with Sunday School friends and cousins but during most of the waiting time we plagued mother with the usual children's questions - "Will they be coming soon mammy? "Will we see daddy, will he be on our side of the road?"

The first banner could be seen coming up 'the line' as a backdrop to the quick stepping flute band and soon the parade was on its way. People closed in shoulder to shoulder to see the bands and the marchers. Mother pushed us in front of her. I liked the pipe bands best as they wore tall black busbies in those days with their swinging kilts. There were girl pipers looking lovely in white frilly blouses. Then the soft toned accordion bands that played hymns.

The banners swung and dipped as they moved along and everyone looked for their own family members amongst the marchers. The spectators often called to marchers whom they knew, "You're looking well William James," and William James waved back at the crowd.

We were intrigued with the pictures of Moses and Gideon's sword on the banners and continued to plague mother with questions. "Why is there a picture of Moses?"

I can still remember being confused on seeing the Bible being carried on a beautiful red velvet cushion and wondered if the story of King William was in the Bible. Had I missed something at Sunday School!

My mother explained as patiently as she could and was probably relieved when the Gloonan Lodge came into view. Our interest was then solely on our own folk and my wee brother and I pushed forward. Two fifers and two Lambeg drummers preceded the lodge. Not much of the drummers could be seen apart from their feet and muscled arms as they waddled along with the huge drum strapped to their stomachs, the sweat streaming down their flushed faces.

The noise was deafening and brought tears to my eyes. I covered my ears but didn't want to move away in case I would miss seeing daddy and my brothers. Uncle Bob was at the front of the procession and he winked across at us. "Why has uncle Bob an apron as well as a sash? Has daddy an apron?"

We continued pestering my mother with questions until she said, "There's the boys," indicating our two brothers stepping along holding the banner tapes and looking neat in their grey short trousers and knee socks. Then daddy was in line with us and he waved as he passed. I felt a sense of pride seeing him dressed and wearing his hard hat and sash. He looked important and much nicer than when in his everyday rough shirt and dungarees and unshaven.

The rest of the parade didn't hold the same interest for us. We were anxious to get to the Field to meet up as a family. Soon the crowd fell in behind the last lodge and followed to the field.

We milled around for a time and then mother said anxiously, "Margaret, watch where you're walking," but it was too late. The cowpat looked as innocent as a 'Ballymena biscuit' lying there in the grass but had the consistency of a good pavalova - crisp on the outside and soft in the centre. One of my nice new sandals with the spongy sole sunk into it up to the buckle. I was devastated so I did the only thing I knew how, I howled like a prairie wolf at the moon.

It was only when my father and two brothers appeared that my mother could get me to quieten down. The sandal was cleaned with tufts of grass while daddy went off to get the Twelfth treat - lemonade and Paris buns. We children enjoyed drinking out of the bottles and the fizz came down our noses making us blink and gulp. The Paris buns, speckled on top with coarse-grained sugar, seemed to taste better than the buns and cakes my mother baked just because they were bought. Then we had ice-cream sliders that we licked round and round between the wafers to keep up with the rate of melting and dribbling. I soon forgot about the sandal. In the distance the voices of the platform party could be heard but no one except the dedicated few cared what was being said. Father lay back on the grass content to be away from the farm for a day and mother sat contentedly watching as we children played around her.

A movement across the field signalled the rest was over and the bands and lodges began to reassemble. The field already looked partially empty as the spectators moved out to get a good position to view the return of the parade to the village.

"Look at your hair Margaret, where's your ribbon?" my mother asked. I put my hand up to feel for the ribbon. The piece of string securing the tuft of hair had slid down and the covering ribbon bow was gone. "Oh mammy, I've lost it".

Mother just shook her head resignedly. I pleaded with her to go back to where we had been playing so that we could look for it but she firmly took my hand saying that it would be trodden on by now and continued heading for the field exit. Thoughts of my new pink ribbon being trampled into cow-clap were too much for me and I started bawling as I trailed alongside her. The lodges were lined up ready to start the return march. As we passed by one of the men standing in a front row with a sword over his shoulder asked, "What's wrong with the wee girl?"

My mother, dignified in spite of my howls, explained that I had lost my ribbon. I looked up at the man sensing a spark of sympathy and sobbed, "It was a new pink ribbon to match my socks."

"Sure here's a far nicer ribbon," he said as he untied the streamers from the handle of his sword and reached them to me. There were actually two ribbons - an orange one and a purple one! My mother graciously smiled and thanked him. Immediately my world changed and I danced excitedly to show my wee brother, who had ignored me throughout my yammering, the two ribbons, I would be the only one at school with an orange and purple bow in my hair. It had been a great Twelfth day after all.

Now when I attend an Ulster-Scots event and watch wee Willie Drennan blatter the Lambeg I have heart-tugging memories of the magic, the music, the colour and carnival atmosphere of my childhood Twelfths.

Margaret Cameron, Belfast

Fever Pitch

I remember one 12th of July in particular, I was 10-years-old at the time. The middle child of five children. Two brothers who were older than me and two sisters who were younger. We were a close knit family, mum and dad made sure we looked out for one another.

The street where I lived in Donaghadee had been decorated with red, white and blue bunting and the flags were blowing gently in the summer breeze. It was a great day for us youngsters and we could hardly wait for the parades and bands to come down our street. But lo and behold, on the 11th of July, I felt poorly. Mum sent for the doctor and I landed in Newtownards Hospital where it was confirmed I had scarlet fever. I cried my eyes out. I missed my family and my sister Dorothy.

But the next day on the 12th of July Dorothy was admitted with scarlet fever too. I remember sitting up in bed and the nurses tied red, white and blue ribbons in our hair. The worst of the fever had gone and it wasn't long till we were home again. But I remember that 12th of July like it was yesterday.

The Twelfth was a family day and relatives would come from far and wide to celebrate it. People really enjoyed the day and talked about it and the grand time they had.

We all got new clothes and wore them with pride and talked about the Twelfth for many a day after.

Margaret Reid, Bangor

The Tweltfh in County Antrim

On 5th July 1947 the brethren of Macartney's True Blues L.O.L 913 Lavin unfurled and dedicated their first banner. The banner replaced a flag which had been carried at the front of the lodge at Battle of the Boyne demonstrations since 1934, and prior to that date flags had been used as standard at the head of the lodge. As a young girl in my mid teens I was extremely pleased and delighted when I was asked along with my three female friends to carry the tapes of the banner, or to give the tapes their proper title of steadying ropes, both at the unfurling ceremony and also on the Twelfth.

The lodge and Lavin Flute Band were so pleased with the achievement of the new banner they decided and agreed to walk to the Twelfth of July demonstration which was in a week's time in the village of Cloughmills a distance of 4.5 miles. Early on the Twelfth morning, the lodge, flute band and supporters left Lavin Orange Hall in North Antrim on foot for Cloughmills taking the route past Ballyweaney Presbyterian Church. A short time after the lodge, band and supporters had left the Orange Hall it was discovered that the parade was being followed by a dog. The dog was immediately identified as a collie dog with the name 'Nellie' which was the pet of a family, and both husband, wife and small family were taking part in the parade. Efforts were made to entice the dog to return to its home but it was so defiant to continue following the crowd and remained with the Lavin party all day. It was the young children from the dog's household that the dog was determined to keep in company with. At some stage en route someone tied an orange and blue ribbon around the dog's neck and it trotted along to the beat of the band drum.

When about half way to Cloughmills a stop was made at the home of Brother Isaac Murphy and his wife Jeannie, and next door was the home of brother Robert Kirkpatrick and his wife Mary. Apart from stopping for a short rest the main reason for the stop was a very welcome meal of tea, sandwiches, buns, fruit loaf and minerals. Everyone just sat by the roadside and thoroughly enjoyed the picnic which was supplied by the lodge and band members, their wives, girlfriends and other well-wishers. In those days it was customary for lodges to be accompanied to and from Twelfth demonstrations by an R.U.C constable. On this occasion the constable who accompanied our party brought his bicycle along. After he availed of the refreshments he got on his bicycle and rode to Cloughmills ahead of our party and met us in the village when our party arrived.

After a short period of relaxation the contingent continued to the village of Cloughmills and made its way to the assembly field in preparation for the main procession to commemorate the Battle of the Boyne. Having taken up position with Ballmoney District Lodge we all made our way to the demonstration field at Main Street, Cloughmills which is presently the location of Cloughmills Memorial Orange Hall.

After the platform proceedings, and meeting up with old acquaintances, it was on the road again for the return walk to Lavin. Everyone had a most enjoyable day and after refreshments in the hall there was a 'social hour, which included old time dancing with music being supplied by Brother James Neill on the mouth organ and accordion. Some complained of being exhausted and fatigued after the Twelfth celebrations but this did not deter them from an early rise on the morning of the 13th July and cycle to Dunloy Railway Station to catch a train for Portrush. Portrush in those days was a most popular place on July 13, one of the main attractions was Duffy's Circus and of course Barry's.

May Gage, Cloughmills

Memories of the Twelfth of July - 70 years ago

My late husband who played the piccolo pictured with our daughter, now aged 17

I was a child of nine or 10 growing up in the country very near Glenkeen Orange Hall in Co. Londonderry. Two highlights of my life were the 12th of July and the Annual Sunday School Excursion. My two brothers and I got very excited about the 12th of July. My brothers looked forward to carrying the tapes of the lovely banner - Glenkeen LOL No. 360. My father was the secretary of this lodge for a number of years. Mother, me and my two brothers got dressed in our best after getting father well creased and dusted down, with his sash exactly perfect.

Off we went to meet at the Orange Hall, and music preceded us down the road about 1/2-mile to the local doctor's house. His wife was an invalid confined to bed and always looked forward to the visit of the band to play her favourite hymn. Then on down the road to meet Agivey Lodge and their lovely pipe band turning out to escort them to the station. We met Ballygawley band and lodge then proceeded on to meet Battlehill band and lodge. It was a lovely sight to see them all coming to board the train at Aghadowey station meeting old friends not seen since the previous year, the hand shakes were many and sincere.

Most mothers and daughters returned home to do the chores, many were farmers. A special evening meal was always prepared for the home coming.

Then we set off to meet the train coming home, each one looking

"I hope when the boss does his King Billy this Twelfth, we're not in front of the

for their own crowd 'which were very special'.

When we came to the hall, we children each got a bottle of lemonade (a rare treat in those days). The chaplain made a nice prayer, the band played 'God Save the King', then home to a happy meal and a wee bag of sweets each from dad. Much chatter and loving gestures brought us to the end of a perfect day.

Mrs May Jamieson, Garvagh

Glenkeen band in the early 1940s

County Fermanagh and the Twelfth

At one time in the Co. Fermanagh countryside there were three "Big Days" every summer. The largest and most important of these occasions was, of course, the Orange parade on the Twelfth of July. Everyone was looking forward for weeks to getting a day in Enniskillen and enjoying some treats, particularly ice cream, which they would get only once or twice in the year.

The second noteworthy event was the celebration on the 29th June for the feast of Saint Peter and Saint Paul when there were bands and marching youth organisations enjoyed by our Catholic neighbours, who were having their "Big Day". However, the reigning Pope at that time, some 40 or 50 years ago, decided that there were too many holidays and banned the celebrations on the 29th of June.

The other important public occasion at the end of August was the Fermanagh County Show with the best livestock on parade at the Fair Green, later the site of the Ulster Farmers' Mart and now occupied by Dunne's supermarket.

The parades on the Twelfth at Enniskillen were by far the largest in the west of the province, attracting large crowds from all around, particularly the border counties of Monaghan, Leitrim, Cavan and Donegal. Large contingents with their bands and banners came by train, by bus, and pony and traps because there were not many private cars on the roads at that time.

Family groups would set off early to walk four or five miles to the County town. Farmers would frequently put a few bags of hay in a farm cart to make seats for the family. When they reached town there were several yards where they could unharness the horse and put him in a stable, safe for the day.

The stabling charge was just a few pence.

The Twelfth would be a subject of discussion in our family for weeks before. There would be speculation about the number of bands and lodges coming, and if there would be three or four Lambeg drummers. In those days a few of the "big drummers" came from around Clones or Newtownbutler, while several would come from the east of the province, possibly Co. Armagh.

About that time, in the early 1930s, a moderately successful farmer would march his growing sons into the family draper's shop in town and order them new suits for The Twelfth. Generally they were made from sturdy tweed, possibly woven in Henderson and Eadie's woollen mills at Lisbellaw.

My mother gave me a new pair of shoes with straps and buckles which I was not allowed to wear before the big day in case they would be spoiled. (More about my new shoes a little later.) When I was a youngster just coming out of childhood, my parents agreed that I was old enough to go to The Twelfth in Enniskillen. I was thrilled at the prospect of getting to town, seeing all the decorations and the shop windows.

My father had a one-day holiday from his job driving a steam roller for the County Council. My mother dressed me in a blue blazer, short pants and stockings. When we were ready to go I was put on the pillion seat of my father's old B.S.A. 250 motorcycle and told to hold fast. Mother waved us off, hoping we would have a good day. She did not want to go. She found the sound of the bands, particularly those Lambeg drums, rather trying.

As we approached the town there were large numbers of red, white and blue flags and colourful streamers across the road. My father stopped and asked at one of the houses if he could leave his motorbike. We walked towards the town centre. I noticed many more streamers and a large arch over the roadway with a loyal slogan on it.

We stopped to watch bands coming out from the railway station. There was a variety of uniforms and young women musicians in several bands. They were playing flutes or melodions. People were seeking out vantage points to get a good view of the procession. In a few places they found grassy banks. Some families brought picnic baskets and flasks of tea.

As my father and I moved on we noticed that in addition to the normal eating houses there were various places serving meat teas and sandwiches. The Orange Hall was doing an excellent trade, serving the bandsmen and women, and the members of the lodges. It was a colourful scene as the brethren wearing their Orange sashes made their way to the assembly point. There were some going on parade wearing bowler hats and white gloves.

Eventually the parade began. The honour of leading it was given to one of the lodges and a band from a border county. It was an impressive sight as the parade marched to popular tunes.

It took over an hour for the long procession to pass. Afterwards my father took me into a restaurant where I had sliced roast beef and a salad. It was tasty. In spite of the meal I began to feel tired and weary.

As a result of all the walking and standing around, my new shoes began to feel very tight. When I tried to walk, it seemed like sharp-pointed nails were coming up through the souls.

When I tried to keep up with my father as we walked back to where he had left his motorbike, my feet became very painful. Each step was a torture.

When I began moaning and crying, my father was angry. He said "Come along. It's not far. Don't be keeping us back." He became even more angry when I begged to be let take off my shoes and walk in bare feet, as I often did at home during school holidays.

"No," he shouted furiously. "What do you think the neighbours would say about you going to the 'Twelfth' in your bare feet. Come on."

I hobbled painfully after him. Some women saw me and said: "Ah, look at the poor child, not fit to walk." My father chastised them. "Mind your own business."

My shoes had become so tight I was in agony. I stopped, crying in sheer pain. Eventually my father relented.

"Oh, all right. Take your shoes off," he said gruffly. I found pure delight and in a short time was able to keep up with my dad for the last half-mile to the motorbike, carrying the torturous shoes by the lacings.

The Twelfth was over but the memory of that painful day remained for a long time.

Mervyn Dane, Enniskillen

Childhood Memories

When I was a child part of the summer ritual was to watch as my mother made a picnic for the Twelfth. Banana or jam sandwiches for us children, ham or egg for the adults. Every year mum would wrap these in tin foil that had been smoothed for the purpose. Then she would arrange them in an empty biscuit tin which was sealed until lunch-time.

I also remember a bottle of diluted juice, flasks for tea, jammy dodgers and crisps. All of these would be packed, along with the biscuit tin, into a woven basket and left at the back door for my dad to put in the car. It was his job to hunt out the striped canvas chair for granny and the rug for us and to pack these also.

In the seventies and early eighties we travelled all over; locally, Loughgall, or Portadown. Sometimes we went further afield to Benburb, or Castlecaulfield where granny lived. But whatever the weather we parked on a farmer's land, avoided the cow pats, searched for the joke stalls before, finally, we chose a spot to watch the parade pass by.

My dad was not an Orangeman, but his father had been. On Sunday afternoons my sister and I would creep into granny's front room, its blue drapes drawn, where, in whispered silence, we examined our grandfather's sash. It was faded orange and as we lifted it out it came with a particular smell that accompanies old and beautiful things. I do not recall a bowler hat or white gloves; just the sash.

One year, in Castlecaulfield, as my little cousin slept in his buggy, I stood in the crowds as the Twelfth spectacle passed in front of us. At some point I realised that Lambeg drums were approaching and I wondered whether I should push the buggy further away to preserve my cousin's sleep. But I was captured by their noise and I remember when, for a brief moment, the three drums aligned with me, my heart thundered in unison with them. After a recent parade my son told me how his blood shook when he heard a Lambeg drum and he thought that his heart was about to fall out.

I knew neither of my grandfathers, they had died before I was born, but mum told me the story of how her father insisted he was a direct descendant of Wilson of the Dyan. Wilson of the Dyan, spoken out loud it has a certain ring to it. The curious thing is that I grew up near the Diamond, yet my immediate family has no direct connection to the area. After 30 years my parents, siblings and I are still regarded as blow-ins by the natives.

Our home was once owned by a man who, as another story goes, donated land to Dan Winter's lodge. Somewhere, there is a photograph, people dressed in an old-fashioned way, which shows this man and the members of the lodge. It was taken in front of our house. Dan Winter's lodge continues to meet in the same place and in the run up to the Twelfth I listen to the sound of rattling Lambegs and my heart beats a little quicker.

In my early twenties I ended up studying in Dublin. Perhaps not an obvious route for a girl to take, having grown up three miles outside Portadown and being a former member of the Drumcree Girls' Brigade. It was a great experience and while there two important things happened. The IRA called a ceasefire and the Drumcree crisis unfolded. My new friends wanted to know what I thought about both, but mostly it was about Drumcree. Many of them knew no one from Northern Ireland and, as far as they were concerned, I was the closest thing to an Orangeman they could find. The trouble was I was unsure how best to articulate the Orangemen's point of view as, at the time, they did not articulate it themselves. Neighbours and relatives had told me about the hurt that was felt and the anger too, but when Drumcree exploded and children died, I could no longer defend something I did not completely understand.

I remember one year before the Twelfth, a friend and I flew over Portadown. He had a pilot's licence and we tracked the motorway until we branched off for the town and I searched below for familiar landmarks. Drumcree, a magnificent church, was nevertheless difficult to spot from the sky. When I found it we flew up the Garvaghy Road, and we had a bird's eye-view of what the rest of the world was seeing through their televisions. I will never forget the protestors who lined along one side of the road and the journalists who lined the other. Later in the week, barbed fence and barricades would keep two communities isolated from each other. Things have calmed down in recent years although matters are far from being resolved. I heard recently that people are now willing to talk and I hope that a way forward for both sides may be found.

I remain curious about Orangeism and would like to understand it better. It is part of my heritage. However, I have always felt that I stood on the periphery of it, at the edge of the parade, so to speak, looking on. One last recollection might illustrate this best of all.

On a crisp September day in 1995 I headed up our hill, camera slung over my shoulder. If it is clear when you reach the top you can see the Sperrins, and if you look back, the Mournes. At night, the lights of Portadown twinkle, and in the distance, during the day, you can hear the gentle hum of traffic, as it makes its way along the Loughgall Road.

It was early morning as I made my way to the corrugated hut that serves as the hall for Dan Winter's Orange Lodge. In 1795 he was a prominent participant in the battle of the Diamond and his descendants can be found living at the site of the battle itself. In fact, I went to school with them. The battle or skirmish, depending on whom you ask, precipitated the creation of the Orange Order in Ireland. Dan Winter, Wilson of the Dyan, they were both involved.

As I climbed the hill in the heart of County Armagh I was struck by how quiet the country was that day. I realised that many would have already gathered at the tiny, tin hut and not even a dog barked as I walked along.

Excited at the thought of catching some history on film, I followed the sweep of the road, first to the left and then to the right until I caught a glimpse of black bowlered heads bobbing along the lane below. In order to get a better view I pulled myself up onto a weathered fence which wavered under my weight. I steadied myself and raised the camera.

Through the lens the front of the hall was visible and I could see that the door was open. In the lane up to the hut and in the space adjacent to it my neighbours were chatting. Clean-shaven and crisply ironed Dan Winter's men were decked out in all their glory as they waited for a signal to form the two parallel lines which would take them to the head of the parade. It was 200 years from the creation of the Orange Order and for this bicentennial commemorative march they were due to take their rightful place at the front. Two hundred years ago they were denied that privilege when others outside the district had taken the title of Loyal Orange Lodge One away from them. In 1995 that wrong was righted by a gesture.

The unmistakable sound of a Lambeg drum began to resonate from the little enclave created by the surrounding drumlins. A heart quickening, thumping beat which lost none of its impact as it travelled up the hill to meet me. I let the camera fall away to see for myself what was happening.

The drum urged the men to take their places. The intensity of the drumming increased until it was no longer a beat but a rabble rousing rattle on hard skin. It reached a crescendo, then stopped. I raised the camera again. Finally, to the rhythm of a solitary beat the participants took a collective breath and stepped forward in unison and I snapped the unfolding drama.

Along ancient hedgerows the marchers moved forward, choreographed by an unseen architect and the drum. An Orange banner, hoisted high, fluttered in a light breeze and the whole ensemble advanced forward, reached the end of the lane, rounded the corner, turned left and proceeded up the opposite hill.

I stopped taking pictures as the procession moved away and decided not to follow them. Instead, I turned around and walked back home thinking how I admired these men for maintaining their tradition.

The photographs lie forgotten in a drawer and I haven't looked at them in years. However, when I think about them and picture them in my mind's eye, the men are marching home and do not look at all out of place in the surrounding countryside.

Nicole Lappin, Portadown

The Grand Orange Field

It's 6am again! I strike my alarm quickly almost knocking it over onto the floor with joy spreading across my face into a beautiful bright smile. I jump out of bed full of enthusiasm and adrenalin pumping around my heart making me feel like a five year-old child all over again. To this day I still get the same happy glow every Twelfth morning.

My first ever memory of this old and beautiful Orange tradition involves my mother dressing me in the prettiest outfit possible. Fashion always makes a strong statement even today for my Twelfth outfit!

Once the whole house was up, bathed and ready to go, my two brothers and I would wait anxiously in the living room for my father to come proudly stepping down the stairs in his crisp white shirt, band tie, kilt and shiny black shoes with bagpipes in tow. He looked so smart and we were one happy family heading to the band hall.

The journey was a mere 10 minutes away but felt like hours! All the way we urged dad to hurry up so we could get to hold some of the strings again. Sometimes we had to wait for the tall old man in his grey shiny suit and golden sash to take us over to the banner before we could pick a string. We felt so proud being escorted to the banner as the pipes and drums practised in the background. Getting to hold a string of the large elegant colourful banners and lead dad's band into the demonstration field was the greatest feeling ever. For us it was like holding onto a balloon you never wanted to let go of. We thought we were little kings and queens at the front of the band.

My mum always went to pick our grandmother Maggie up. She also dressed for the occasion in her pale blue or white, almost business like skirt suits with her gold clasped handbag on arm. She was like the royalty of the spectators to me, the crowning glory in making my day feel special. She would watch out for us marching towards her and mum, both waving at us as we entered the big field with the sun dancing to our every move and beat of the big bass drum.

The field was our favourite part of the day. The band bring their sweet music to a close while marching on the spot at their little white lodge numbered signpost. We knew then we would go with dad down to the field's entrance to meet up with mum and granny. We then got a juicy burger to eat and a can of coke. We would then sit back in the Orange field enjoying our food and the spectacle of all the other bands and lodges entering into the grand field.

It was great being with mum and gran, they took us to all the band stalls spread out along the back length of the field. It took us a while to get round them all but every step was worth the prizes or little gadgets we returned with, bought specially for us by the people we love.

Sometimes I would get badges, a flag and bubbles to blow, whereas the boys would get drums, band sticks or noisy bouncy balloons to play with. All of which mum had to carry home for us naturally.

We stayed there playing for hours enjoying every moment before dad would return, pick us up and make our way back to the band's designated spot. How he managed to find us among all those crowds of people we will never know.

The band warmed up their bagpipes in their steadfast circle playing the Rowntree, a tune that will stay with me always as the tune from the field. The boys, my cousins and I would run after each other around the circle playing tig until we all fell dizzy in a pile on top of one another bursting into fits of giggles, trying to get our breaths back before going to get more much needed free lemonades from the lodge.

The band's leaving of the Orange field always made me realise that the big day was almost over and that we would soon be on our way back home on the buses to where we started. Still, I gladly put on my best smile, made sure my white sandals were clean and free from any grass and danced with the band and banner as the lodge men swayed it back and forward under the trees even when we were heading up the long hill to the band hall in County Tyrone.

Then finally, on stopping outside the hall, everything became still and quiet as the band piped our country's national anthem 'The Queen' with two strikes of the drum. Then our day trip would all be over, apart from the party that night, but that's another memorable story all on its own.

Annette Kirk, Dungannon

Twelfth Memories

I remember beautiful, bright, colourful Twelfth days back in the 1950s, Which started very early in the morning for my sister Patricia and I. We would suddenly awake to the sound of the first flute band leaving the newly built Whiterock Orange Hall.

This would cause us to jump out of bed and rush to the window of our West Circular Road home, to watch the handsome young men in their smart uniforms pass by.

Then it would be all systems go to get ourselves ready. Put on our new dresses and sandals, not forgetting the "kiss me quick" hats, pick up the sandwiches our mother had left ready, then out the door as fast as we could to catch the bus, along with loads of other people.

The buses would be packed solid. We would make our way to Carlisle Circus Orange Hall, where we would meet up with cousins and friends alike. This was where the lodges and many of the bands from our side of the town would gather and then set off from.

We teenagers would choose one of the liveliest bands to walk and indeed dance alongside, all the way to the field at Finaghy and back. I think it was a distance of about seven miles. I remember once buying a punnet of delicious ripe strawberries costing sixpence, also a red, white and blue streamer for three pence to wave at the boys.

This photograph which was taken at "The Field" in the early 1950s shows my grandfather Alex, my mother and father and myself in the middle along with my brother and sister. A good day was had by all!

When we finally reached the field, we would head for the nearest tent to buy ice cream and lemonade. Buns and sandwiches were also available for the hungry revellers.

We had many relatives and friends amongst the men who walked in the lodges. So we always stood along the roadside at the end of our journey to watch all the different districts pass by, calling out the names of this one and that one to make sure they saw us and waved back. That was all part of the fun. Indeed each Twelfth day was always special in one way or another. The fun we had, the friendships we formed which stayed in our memories long after. It was all so colourful and lively. Those huge banners which two men had to carry, with beautiful pictures depicting events from history, such as famous battles, Bible story pictures of David and Goliath, shipwrecks, even paintings of famous Ulster men who had passed on.

Then there were also the Orange Lodges from far away places such as Africa, Canada and New Zealand.

Of course the Scottish bands were always met with great applause by the bystanders, as they always seemed to make that extra effort when beating the drums and banging the cymbals together to make as much noise as possible.

The sweat would be lashing off the men who carried those huge Lambeg drums beating away at them with those strange bent bamboo drum sticks. They were a particular favourite of mine. I never failed to be amazed at how skilful those muscular men with their bleeding knuckles were. Not least, because my own grandfather, Alex Cairns owned two of those big drums in his day.

The story in the family goes that during the First World War, when granda was off fighting at the Battle of the Somme, he sent a postcard home to granny which said, "Don't forget to turn the drums". Nothing else not even a loving sentiment.

It seems he kept two of those great drums hung up on pullies at the top of the stairs in a kitchen house in Suir Street, Belfast. Apparently as soon as Alex arrived home from war, having been the only man in the family to arrive home safe and well, he took one of the drums up to the corner of the street and beat the living daylights out of it to the amusement of the gathering crowd. So delighted was he to have survived the war and got back to his wife and family.

A few weeks later he went down to the recruitment office and re-enlisted with the Royal Engineers Labour Squad and went back to Flanders Fields to help bury the dead. He could not rest and was plagued by nightmares of the awful atrocities he had witnessed, he felt he had to return.

He lived until his 83rd year and told his grandchildren that there was never a day passed when he did not think of his pals who fell at the front.

Margaret Steed, Greyabbey

Childhood Memories of the Twelfth

As I sit in my armchair now an invalid, my mind races back to my childhood days. Born in 1933 I have seen many changes in my lifetime. As we come to this time of year and the 1st of July is upon us, my mind always goes back to the days when I was young and we all looked forward so much to the Twelfth of July. As I am travelling through the countryside and see the hedges being cut and smell the fresh cut grass it reminds me of how it was back then, people would start preparing for the Twelfth celebrations.

The hay was made, potatoes were sprayed, carts were painted blue and their wheels were done with orange lead paint, I don't believe there is such a thing on the market nowadays. The out-houses were cleaned out leaving them ready for the harvest and a bonfire made and set alight. The outside walls were then whitewashed and a skirting of tar was put around the bottom of the house to leave a nice finish and to preserve the whitewashed walls. Inside the house got the same makeover. Decorating the walls, washing blankets and quilts all done by hand, getting the flour bags washed and bleached, ready for making sheets, bolsters and pillowslips in the longer winter evenings.

I was just six years old when the Second World War broke out bringing our country to a standstill. The government passed a law that all large assemblies and gatherings were to be banned and a lot of our men went off to fight the war and indeed some of the women in our area went also. We had to be satisfied with picnics or fetes held at the church but we all enjoyed them. It was a day out and we had plenty of fun. At one particular outing as a treat King Billy arrived on his horse. As children we believed it was really him and to this day I still think about it. We were not short of fun although everyone was glad when the Twelfth returned.

This law was to last for the next six years. In 1945 the war was over and it was as if a cloud had been lifted and the sun had come through again.

It was a new dawn, the Twelfth of July was on again and I was 12. When I was six it was the highlight of the day to be allowed to carry the strings of the banner. You had to take your turn to do this as there were a lot of children in the lodge and only four could do it at once. Now that I was 12 carrying the strings didn't seem as interesting as I was beginning to have an eye for the boys, but my mother made sure I still took my turn.

I looked forward to the Twelfth with anticipation. The band started to practice about two or three months beforehand-not as sophisticated as nowadays. An odd wrong note didn't matter and of course some dummy fluters helped to swell the numbers. I never could play the flute, sure girls were not popular in bands at that time. There were plenty of other things they could do to help the day go with a swing – make sandwiches, sweep the floors, helping to put the Orange Lilies and Sweet William on the drums, the buzz was tremendous.

On the eleventh night the wives of the Orangemen would gather at the hall to make sandwiches for everyone coming home from the Twelfth. It was also quite a highlight, everyone looked forward to this part. Although the war was over, food and clothes were still rationed and there was always nice sweet tea. That is one of my fondest memories and something I enjoy even to this present day. And then what better place to get ham for the sandwiches than the 'Free State'. We lived near the border so some of the members would happily go off earlier that evening to get the ham and maybe a drink or two. No mention then about drinking and driving.

On one particular night the ham didn't arrive back until midnight and I don't have to tell you what the women had to say, but the sandwiches were still made and left ready for the next day. An old trick or two had to be played, such as putting a piece of brown paper in instead of ham, setting it up for someone who had a 'short fuse', Nobody wanted to go to bed on the Eleventh Night, it was all too exciting. The Twelfth morning had arrived and we all got dressed in our Sunday best. My father always asked a Catholic gentleman to milk the cows and feed the hens and pigs and gather the eggs. This gave us time to enjoy the day. The whole family would walk to the Orange Hall. It would take about 15 minutes to get there and we would call in on our way for our neighbours who played in the band. We were all so excited.

What an array of colours, everyone was dressed to kill. The bandsmen had no uniform but wore their Sunday best, and when they put on their sashes they all looked a million dollars. The band would strike up the 'Sash' and march up the narrow country road followed by the Orangemen and last of all the women and children. The buses would sit at the top of the road and wait for their load. The women and children would get on first and the Orangemen would roll up the banner and carefully put it in through the window of the bus and off they would go.

When we arrived at the venue the band and Orangemen had to wait for the formation of the other lodges for the march to the field. When we arrived at the field we always looked forward to getting tea and sandwiches at one of the tents. There were tents with food and other stalls but it didn't matter to me because I had very little money and had to keep it for food. With my friends we would start to walk around and enjoy the day always on the look out for a boy and usually we weren't disappointed. Then in the distance you could hear the speeches begin. We never went over to listen to them and anyway we couldn't have cared less what they were saying. All we wanted to do was enjoy the day. Then the bands and lodges that were in the field earlier would start to leave and we would watch this, and then it would be our turn and we would all head back to the buses, but the day wasn't over yet. When we got back to the hall everyone got off at the top of the road and the band would strike up again and march back down the narrow road to the hall. The sandwiches were then distributed. The corners turned up with the heat and we got a bottle of warm lemonade.

The pastries were hard and tasteless, but sure I didn't mind. I had fun with the rest of the boys and girls from other families while the men sat around drinking a bottle of stout and making their craic. The Twelfth was over for another year and we were looking forward to the next. What I would give now to have it all back again but alas it is gone forever.

Margaret Brown, Armagh

My Father's Bowler Hat

The Twelfth is fast approaching and thus starts the flurry of church services. As I take down my father's bowler from the top shelf of the wardrobe, switch on the electric kettle and start to steam the hat so that the felt takes on a new lease of life, I can't help but notice the name of the hatter proudly stamped within, J Baird Hatter, Mayfair, Belfast.

I let my mind wander down the paths of years long since gone, to the first Twelfth of July that as a very small boy I accompanied my father to Lisburn. I remember my mother say that she would not be at home when we returned. On the way to Lisburn my father said not to worry, my mother would be there when we returned and that she would never leave us. That Twelfth I walked with my father wearing a small Orange collarette. I felt safe holding onto my father's hand as the bands played and the banners fluttered in the gentle summer breeze. That was the only time I paraded with my father as he died the following year at a comparatively young age leaving my mother a young widow left to bring up two sons on her own.

In those far off days I remember helping collect wood for the bonfire and getting into trouble with my mother for being late home for tea. Then there was the eleventh night when the bonfire was lit. The adults would dance in the street to the sound of someone's gramophone which was perched precariously on a window sill and we the children would be allowed to stay up a little longer to watch the festivities. Then came the Twelfth morning. We arose early and went to the dying embers of the bonfire armed with potatoes which we baked in the last heat of the fire. After eating the potatoes which tasted delicious, my friends and I, for a sixpence each paid by our parents, carried chairs up to the front of the Lisburn Road and sat on them until our parents and relatives from the country arrived to take up their places for the parade.

Those were good days to remember, I hadn't mentioned that the two boys who helped with the chairs were Catholic. That didn't appear to matter as the neighbours in the avenue were mixed and everyone went up to the top of the avenue to watch the Orange Order and the bands parade past on their way to the field. We spent the sixpence on lemonade and ice cream as we sat on the kerb and watched the parade go by. Then in the evening we earned another sixpence if we sat on the chairs until the adults returned for the parade to pass on its way from the field, I reflected that cross community co-operation is not a new word. It was working well in those bygone days when things weren't too plentiful and when one woman's husband was out of work another would make a big black pot of soup or stew and place some in a smaller pot and take it over to the neighbour's house.

O.J. Hamill L.O.L. 1970, Belfast

Ballyroney LOL 300

I WAS brought up in a family of four children, three girls and one boy. From an early age the Twelfth of July was a major event in our family's social calendar. Even the lead up to the Twelfth was filled with excitement. There was the bonfire night on the 11th of July, the putting up of the arch and the annual Sunday pre-Twelfth service at the church to look forward to. On the 1st of July the Union Jack had to be put up. My father brought the flag down from the loft and dusted off the cobwebs before displaying it on the hayshed roof. There was always a competition to see which of our neighbours would have their flag up first. The arch was also put up on the 1st of July. The lodge members of Ballyroney LOL 300, the lodge my father was in, gathered at night to put up the arch. I used to enjoy watching the men heaving up the arch with the aid of ladders, forklifts and lorries. When the arch was up we all used to admire King Billy on his horse with the letters 'Ballyroney LOL 300' in the background.

The Twelfth morning was always a hectic one. Dad was up at 7am to get ready for the parade. He was pole bearer so he had to make sure everything was in order for the parade.

The lodge gathered at Ballyroney Orange Hall around 10.30am. They paraded to Ballyroney Bridge accompanied by Moneyslane Accordion Band and back to the hall. The bus arrived at 11am to take the men to the demonstration field. I used to enjoy the bus journey to the field with my dad. Mum and the rest of the family travelled in the silver Ford Cortina to the field.

The parade got underway around 12pm. Each lodge marched with their own band. I have been to many Twelfths, but the one I remember well was in our home town of Rathfriland 'on the hill'. We hadn't far to travel that year, only three miles. The assembly field was on the Castlewellan Road and we had to walk 1 1/2 miles to the demonstration field just on the outskirts of the town. I walked beside dad as he was carrying the pole. The procession was made up of all types of bands, accordion, flute, pipes etc. I loved the flute bands or as we call them, the blood and thunder. You could hear them playing for miles. The drummer was beating the big drum so loud you thought it was going to explode. The louder the crowd cheered, the harder he beat the drum. I would always have loved to have been in an accordion band but was never musically minded. As we marched along the route, we were cheered along by hundreds of spectators, some wearing union hats, whilst others waved Union Jacks. The march took approx. one hour to get from the assembly field to the demonstration field. We couldn't wait to get to the field to rest our legs after the long journey. When we arrived at the field the atmosphere was buzzing with entertainment for young and old. There were bouncy castles, face painting, poker machines, amusement arcades, ice-cream vans, chip vans, food tents, marquees selling tapes, toys etc.

All the lodges marched up to the platform party and remained there until the service was over. The platform party was made up of District Masters plus clergy. The service lasted half an hour with a band playing a few hymns.

After the service was over everyone was queuing at food tents to get something to eat. Our lodge queued up at the Ballyward tent where we got hot tea, sandwiches and buns. Everyone was so glad to get a seat. Some of the men even lay down on the grass and fell asleep.

The march back took approx. one hour. When we had finished the journey the buses were waiting to take us back to the Orange Hall. When we arrived back, there was a big barbecue for everyone, laid on by the ladies of the lodge.

My memories of the Twelfth were always happy ones and I hope my children will have the same memories as me.

Mrs Olive Dobson, Cookstown

Twelfth Memories

My parents never went to the Twelfth Demonstration as there were too many of us at home to get ready. There were 14 in one family and life was hard work on the farm from dawn till dusk.

My mother was always busy baking bread on the griddle, at the church making butter or making clothes for us to wear while my father tended to the animals and kept the horses in peak condition. It was hard work to earn a living in those days.

However, 70 years ago my sister and I had our first experience of the Twelfth. We were so excited we could hardly get to sleep the night before.

An old lady by the name of Anita Petticrew - a friend of our family who also lived in Drumcaw - between Castlewellan and Clough, took us out for the day.

There was an Orange Hall in Drumcaw and a large number of men in the lodge there. They also had a flute band. Two of my brothers played flutes in the band, and it was great to see them all dressed up and wearing their sashes on the Twelfth morning. They were immaculate in their dress for the occasion. We were very proud of them.

The lodge was going to Comber and to me that was like going abroad. There were buses provided to take the band and lodge to Comber and we went on a bus as well with Anita. Oh what a wonderful day it was, the sun was splitting the trees. Watching all the bands and banners pass was truly spectacular. We'd never seen anything like it before. I also enjoyed the music very much. I always had a good ear for it.

When we got to the field, which seemed like ages, we enjoyed some sandwiches and buns and even chips. We ate like we'd never seen a bite before, this was something truly different. The food was provided by the ladies lodge.

In the field Anita bought us each a lovely blue beret and we couldn't wait to get wearing them and showing them off at home. We were so happy and excited, but then it all turned to tears. In the midst of all the crowds and excitement I lost my nice blue beret. My sister held on tight to hers then in case it would get lost too and I thought maybe I could wear hers as well. We were good at sharing.

Soon it was time for all the bands to get ready for home on the bus again and by that time we were all tired. We had a great day out and I enjoyed it very much apart from the beret getting lost and it was to be my last Twelfth for many a year.

Then on the 10th Sept 1952 I married a Mourne man and saw many Twelfth demonstrations with family and friends in Kilkeel, Annalong and Ballymartin.

I don't bother as much now as I am over 80 years of age and can't get about the same. I depend very much on my family for getting out and about and still see the odd parade but I read a lot and do puzzles and crosswords and keep in touch with what's going on in the News Letter everyday.

Mrs Peggy Nugent, Kilkeel

A Quare day for it

My foot tapped to the rhythm that was older than the history the music was celebrating. The banners and flags waved and fluttered in the wind like weary lumbering spirits returning from some mystical tryst, while the highly polished shoes marched with military precision past the vantage point of the camera, just as it had done for as long as I could remember.

Sitting with me my son asked why I never took him to see 'the bands'. I ignored the question, instead walking into the kitchen to make coffee. I was ashamed I'd deflected the enquiry but I didn't want to get into the explanation of being raised on the other side of the fence', 'left footers' and all the other paraphernalia attached to Ulster politics.

It was later on that the question nagged me so much that I confronted the real reason I couldn't answer my son. Although I was from the other side, well half of me, as my parents were from each division, I had myself in years gone by enjoyed the Twelfth with all the vigour and verve of a native. My father had been in a pipe band and seeing the 'kilties' was a big part of his life and became so for me.

I remembered he was always drumming on any hard flat object with the sticks he kept while showing me photos of himself in his regalia. Memories in sepia of youthful eyes reflecting oceans of hope in a time long before the years of darkness that began in 1969.

As I recalled those days at my father's side the panorama of memory opened up before me like a vast curtain, to an occasion when it seemed bright sun rays blazed out of a cloudless sky, while myriad drums and banners streamed amid a cacophony of drums and flutes and cheering hands, clutching flags, pressed against the throng of marchers.

I remember the sense of anticipation churn up inside me like an espresso machine on the Twelfth morning, an Ulster fry inside me as I sat on the bus, and the short walk from the stop to the front of the City Hall seemed interminable. I pulled at my dad's arm trying to get him to walk faster while away in the distance the gentle thudding noise of the approaching bands increased in volume as we got closer only added to the aura of expectancy.

Once arrived, the heady atmosphere of excitement was as potent as any perfume and there was a real sense of community and belonging on a day out, that in my young years seated at the front of The City Hall, seemed to stretch for ever. My dad, who always seemed to don a tie, had on his summer clothes of open necked shirt, flannels and sandals that were as much the signature of summer to me as a bucket and spade or candy floss.

I could still taste the lemonade and buns and feel the stickiness of the sugar on my fingers wrapped around the thin wooden shaft of my flag as my tireless arm waved and danced the cloth through the air that twanged and reverberated to the music.

Band after band after wonderful band passed, ablaze with colour and pulsating with energy. Flute, accordion and brass bands dressed so smartly they could have walked off the lid of a sweet tin. And of course my dad's favourites - the pipe bands - skirled past like tartan armies, kilts swirling and pipes splitting the air. I thought them a fearsome sight. Huge burly men, red faced from their exertions on the pipes. Then there were the moments of delicious fear I felt at their awesome countenance and I stuck close to my dad as he explained the different drum rhythms.

At the front of each band were the baton twirlers and the crowd were agog at the mastery of their craft. I stood in awe as the coloured stick soared and spun through the air and each time you were convinced he'd drop it but like a washer to a magnet it would be snatched just off the ground by the precision in his catch almost as if he had a homing device attached to his hand.

Hour after hour of spectacle of the procession passed until, all too soon like all good things, it was over and for the next two weeks I walked up and down the garden, throwing brush poles in the air and using wooden spoons to bang a cardboard box that was secured around my neck with coarse string.

Thinking back, I couldn't recall when it all changed save for the perception that one day the colour and pageant was usurped and smeared with a veneer of mistrust. Now instead of a vista of celebration and gaiety, it was as if I was looking at the scene through a soiled opaque glass that distorted the image so the flags became gnarled and vapid and the music brash, triumphalist lacking dignity and integrity. Truths, half-truths and lies were intertwined in a tangled web that choked and manacled the essence event and I admitted to myself that I'd failed to look with objective eyes and was prepared to peer from across the fence and accept what image that suited my dormant prejudice.

It was this prejudice that I wasn't aware of and had never challenged that was the real reason I couldn't answer my sons question. I'd ignored the changes in the past years, avoided the efforts to drive out the rotten apples, and shunned the efforts to restore the day to its former glory. I had put my reasons on trial and had found them lacking.

So now what? Those days, however they were perceived, were fading like the colour of fabric in strong sunshine. Now was the time to stand and be counted and enjoy the day for what it was. Now was the time to take away the glass and let the colour pour back in and once again let the music of the bands add to the rhythm of the new dawn breaking over the province.

Again I was sitting at my father's side and again the sun was hot on my back and the summer holidays were laid out before me like a vast wedding banquet. I knew what my father would have wanted. He wouldn't have brought me anywhere he thought was corrupted or bitter and nor should he have and I could only do the same. My son should enjoy the day out as I had.

I was determined to rekindle the warmth of feelings that I had felt all those years ago and give my son the same opportunity, with the confidence that I could field any historical question he may ask. Of course he probably wouldn't ask as he would enjoy the day for what it was and embrace it as we all should, with the integrity and purity of children.

The next Twelfth arrived and I made good my promise to myself. This was going to be the first time in nearly 40 years I had watched the bands and, as with my father, my son would be by my side as we left the house sustained by potato bread and soda farls.

The sun was growing higher in the sky and in the distance could be heard the telltale rumble of what lay ahead. I said out loud, "You know what son? They're gettin' a quare day for it".

Robert Semple, Belfast

Twelfth Memories

YOU always remember the good ones: the 'Twelfths' when the sun shone and the sky was blue and there wasn't a raincoat or a pac-a-mac or an umbrella in sight.

Like the one when I was a month short of my 13th birthday. It was my first time on parade. A nervous second cornet player in the Bruce Hamilton Memorial Silver Band, rasping out the syncopated counter melody of military marches as I strode out, as manfully as my little legs allowed. In a hand-me-down blue uniform with trousers so ill-fitting they began round my armpits and ended under my shoes, and a hat so large and loose it rested on my ears despite having two pages of the News Letter folded inside in an attempt to make it tighter.

Even so, I was honoured to play for the 'Bruce' - as some brass band aficionados called us - for we were a prize-winning band with a name and a history to be proud of. You see, Sergeant Bruce Hamilton, whose portrait was painted on the front of the bass drum, was a local hero who had paid the supreme sacrifice in one of those bloody battles fought across the fields of Flanders in the Great War.

You knew it was going to be a scorcher as me and my big brother walked into town, for the heat haze was already shimmering over the dips in the road like some phantom mist in a bog. My big brother, who played first cornet and who had been with the band for ages, was well buoyed up for the day ahead. Laughing and joking and treating passing acquaintances to his usual comic turn of posing as a travelling salesman, holding aloft his cornet case and calling out: "Going cheap, all colours of black thread!"

As we arrived in the town square we were bidden a cheery 'Happy Twelfth of July' by the local Non-Subscribing Minister, an Englishman and recent convert to Orangeism. His sombre suit and black Homburg hat colourfully enhanced with a brand new collarette.

The Orange Hall was black with bowlers and shining sashes and Sunday suits with buttonholes of white carnations and pink and purple Sweet William. You could reach out and touch the atmosphere, the cheerfulness, the sense of importance, the feeling that this was the Orange Order's most 'high and holy' day and that something memorable and exciting was about to happen. The sun glinted on swords, and the big lodge banner, hoisted high in the air like a becalmed sail, hardly stirred in the windless morning.

We fell in, the band in front under the command of Drum Major Cyril Whithorn, a veteran of the 1939-45 war. Then the steady beats on the bass drum by William James Ogle and a long, slow, double roll by the side-drummers and we were off. Down Princess Street, under the red, white and blue bunting, blasting out 'Colonel Bogey'. Left right, left right, shoulders back, chest out, under the big Orange arch that spanned the width of the street on the east side of the square, the painting of the Queen way up on the left hand corner and two

The Bruce Hamilton memorial silver band in the 1950s with the President, the late Dr. J.C Wilson holding the Brass band league cup.

To his right is the conductor, the late William Atkinson

model cannons and two blue-painted miniatures of Captain Browning's relief ship the 'Mountjoy' sailing across the top beam.

We were bound for Rathfriland. Which sounded more than a little exotic to my untravelled ears for I had been no further than Banbridge and Belfast and a couple of times to Newcastle on Sunday School excursions. There is only one way to approach Rathfriland. By hill, long and tortuous hills, irrespective of where you've journeyed from. So we fell in at the bottom of the steepest of all the hills, a long crocodile of lodges and Lambeg drums, pipe bands, flute bands accordion bands and brass and silver bands. All sweating freely, for the sun was now at its highest and hottest. We dripped sweat as we played 'Imperial Echoes' and 'The Boys of the Old Brigade', cheeks puffed out with the combined effort of climbing and spitting the notes into cornets, euphoniums and trombones. Our bass tuba player, who would have been about fifty but appeared ancient to my innocent eyes, fell by the wayside with an attack of breathlessness.

So we breasted the hill to the field, marking time now and then as the procession concertinaed and lost momentum. "A bit like climbing Donard", someone said. "As if it will never end". But it did eventually and we flung off caps, loosened tunics, eased belts and braces, and lay on the grass and ate sandwiches and drank sweet tea. Lovers sprawled here and there, oblivious, embracing away the long hot afternoon, and in the distance, a loudspeaker on a flag-bedecked lorry droned its speeches to the somnolent sun.

Rathfriland was a slowly moving scrum of spectators, pipers in kilts, bandsmen in a whole array of uniforms, and off-duty Orange brethren in groups of twos and threes, the gold and silver tassels of carefully-folded collarettes spilling from suit pockets.

That was the year Ruby Murray had seven songs in the 'Hit Parade', and a jukebox in a cafe in the town square poured out: 'Softly, softly, come to me. Touch my lips so tenderly'.

That distinctive husky voice, sounding like it was suffering from an acute case of laryngitis, competing with the cries of street traders selling their wares.

People gorged on fish suppers and dipped anticipatory fingers into bags of chips, and the ice-cream shop ran out of ice-cream.

Then it was time for home. We retrieved musical instruments from the unruly pile on the grass where they had lain unprotected all afternoon, fastened tunics, buckled belts and replaced caps. We paraded round the town square and down the hill to where the green and cream UTA buses waited to take us to Dromore. Back home, we paraded from the Banbridge Road to the Orange Hall. The same spectators who had waved us off in the morning, lining the streets to welcome us home. Then the national anthem on the road in front of the Orange Hall and the 'fall out' and the slow climb up the stairs to the upper room of the hall for ham salad, bread and butter and more tea.

I was foot-sore and worn-out when I reached home and an early bed-time sounded good. But my father had other ideas. "How's about we dander up to the 'Cradle Hall' and see if there's a bit of value?" So I changed my clothes and we walked up the road past Gourley's Loanin and Baxter's Moss to Ballaney Orange Hall with its distinct shape like the old-fashioned child's cradle that gave it its nick-name. You could see the weather changing as we walked. It was hotter than ever, oppressive, muggy, the sky slowly becoming bruised with thunder-clouds.

There was a Twelfth night soiree in the hall and we had tea and buns and people sang. They had to open the windows, their warped wooden frames screeching, to let the Worshipful Master have some air as he sang that lovely old song 'The Shepherd Boy'.

It was dark when we left the hall. Long fingers of lightning flickered across the sky as we walked home and muffled rolls of thunder rumbled in the distance. The first, fat spits of rain began as we reached our gate, and by the time it took to walk the ten steps to the house the rain was drumming on the tarmac off the road.

"Wasn't it great?" said my father, "That you got your first Twelfth over without getting wet."

"We were very lucky, weren't we daddy?" I said, and we went inside and shut the door against the rain.

Roy Gamble, Dromore

The 'Big Day!'

FOR a young schoolboy of nine or ten-years-old, playing on the streets of Ballymena, the Twelfth of July was always a really magical time. We always knew the 'Big Day' was drawing near when we heard the Lambeg drums of 'Galgorm Parks' LOL 507 from the west side of town, being answered by the drummers in Broughshane from the east and just for good measure the Lambegs of Ballymarlow LOL 637 from the south side of town added their staccato beats to the throbbing sound echoing around the Antrim Hills.

We were living in a little cul-de-sac of 32 red brick houses. The lower end of the street was closed off by the rear of High Kirk Presbyterian Church and a store known as the 'Greenvale Produce Store' owned by a Mr Andy Robinson, a generous man who allowed the locals to keep the barrels, poles and frame of the Orange Arch on his premises from year to year. For us children this store became a place of fascination for two or three weeks prior to the Twelfth.

Every night after working hours, all the able bodied men and many of the women would go down to the 'Greenvale Store' to prepare the Arch. The smell of the orange and blue paint for the barrels and the red, white and blue for the poles was really overwhelming.

While the men painted the women would cut the orange and blue paper into some lovely designs to cover the frame of the arch. Then the Orange symbols including 'King William' on his horse would be freshened up.

We children were kept busy with orders from the men. "Go up home and get me some Turpentine!", "Bring down some old rags so we can clean our hands!", "Go to the 'wee shop' and get a packet of Woodbine and be quick about it." We didn't mind one bit as we thought we were really helping out.

As the days passed and the arch took shape our excitement grew, and when all was complete Mr Robinson provided one of his lorries and the barrels, poles and frame were loaded and moved to the centre of the street, everyone was at their door to witness the hoisting of the Arch.

The ropes supporting the Arch were put through the skylights of houses on opposite sides of the street and fastened down. When this task was completed a big cheer went up from all the neighbours.

Then one by one the 'Union Flags' would go out the bedroom windows, no 'Palestine or Israeli Flags', no 'Ulster Flags or Scottish Saltires' in those days. Just the colours of the good old 'Union Standard'. Then the rows of streamers and little Greenvale Street were a riot of colour, but the real moment of pride came on the Twelfth morning, when Craigywarren LOL and their UVF Flute Band formed in 1913, (the only original UVF Band in Ulster) would proudly march down the street stop under the arch and give us a selection of Orange tunes, and this band is still on parade to this day.

Now I would like to move my story forward a few years, when I was 15 years old. I saw our local pipe band the 'Seven Towers' on parade. They had been the official band for the 'Mid-Antrim Home Guard' during the War-years 1939-45.

They wore the 'Cameron Tartan' and khaki battledress tunics and the sound of the pipes and drums really thrilled me. So a pal and I joined the band in May 1946 and on the Twelfth day that year we walked alongside the band to the field as they accompanied 'Ballymena Golden Star LOL 491', and we made a pact that day that we would play in the ranks come the Twelfth 1947. He as a piper and myself as a side-drummer. We kept that pact and for the next 23 years I proudly played in the band as we still led 'Golden Star LOL'. Sadly my piper-pal emigrated to the land of 'Maple Leaf' and was killed in a road traffic accident.

For myself that first Twelfth Parade in 1947 started a love affair with pipe bands that took me to contest fields all over Ireland and Scotland, with many prizes along the way. We as a band took part in RBP parades, and even walked the famous Walls of Londonderry with the Apprentice Boys, and took part in fireworks displays in Portrush. One of my lasting memories of the Twelfth was marching with the 'Seven Towers' from 'Harryville Orange Hall', on the morning of the 'Big Day' to the home of our treasurer and founder member, a Mr Sam Hyndman. He lived down Queen Street in Ballymena. Here we were treated to sandwiches, buns and lemonade, and all the members were given a ten shilling note, big money in those days.

When I went into the ranks of the band in 1947, we were still wearing the original tartan 'Cameron of Erracht' which was chosen when the band was formed in 1926, as a 'thank you' to a generous benefactor a Mr Cameron. We also had 'black tunics' edged with silver braiding and with diamond shaped buttons, bearing a thistle. We had horse hair sporrans and white spots.

As I watch the Twelfth procession these days it saddens me to see that pipe bands have completely departed from the Belfast march, and are fast leaving the town and country parades as well, as they added so much colour and spectacle to the occasion.

Stewart Davison, Ballymena

Twelfth of July Birthday Girl

I could hear the distant sound of a pipe band and my mother was leaning over my bed gently coaxing me to waken up. I rubbed my sleepy eyes and raised my tousled head from my pillow. The sunlight was just beginning to stream in through the leadlight window. Today was the Twelfth of July, my birthday. I had arrived unexpectedly into this world on the Twelfth of July in the morning, four years previously. My Mum had eaten too much yellow man down Sandy Row on the eleventh night and had severe indigestion which turned out to be me.

At four years old I believed that having a birthday on the Twelfth meant that I was the luckiest girl in the entire world because I had the biggest, most wonderful, noisy parade for my birthday. None of my friends could ever have a party like mine!

I could feel the excitement mounting as I was hurriedly washed and dressed and sat down to breakfast. It was very early, about 6.00am but the day had to get underway. Birthday cards and presents were on the table and I hurried to open them. A picture story book, new ribbon for my hair and a surprise half a crown from aunt Sally and uncle Tommy were amongst the presents. I got hugs and kisses from everyone and I just knew it was going to be the best birthday ever.

My grandmother, who I called nanna because she said granny was for old ladies, was fussing around making sandwiches, washing strawberries and she didn't know I saw her hiding a cake and candles in the picnic basket. The kettle was whistling on the boil and the flasks were lined up ready to be filled with tea. Mum was seeing to my little brother.

The sound of the band was louder now because the man three doors away, Mr Anderson, was the master of the lodge. He was very special so the band and all the other Orangemen had come to meet him at his house before joining the big parade. I wasn't sure what Orangemen were but there they stood in rows all wearing their Sunday best with bowler hats, white gloves and well polished shoes. Some of them also had very shiny swords which they held upright and they glistened in the sunlight.

I was a bit afraid of Mr Anderson because he was very tall and was a policeman and he had an Alsatian dog who had tried to bite my hand once. Today he was the leader of my birthday parade so I put my worries aside and went with my grandpa to the gate to see the banner unfurled and hear the drummers beat out the marching rhythm. The bandsmen were all dressed in kilts, hats with plumes, thick white socks and shiny shoes. They squeezed the woolly tartan things under their arms and blew into the long pipes until an agonising sound came out which miraculously became blood stirring music. They had furry things like handbags at the front of their kilts and I wondered if they kept a hanky in there. I always had a clean white hanky but I had to keep it up my sleeve and sometimes it fell out.

Grandpa shouted to Mr Anderson to have a good day and said the weather looked set to be fine and sunny, maybe too hot for a long march but better than rain. Grandpa gestured towards me and told him it was the wee girl's birthday. Mr Anderson flashed me a smile and came down the street and handed me an orange lily. He told me to wear it on my frock that day because I was very special. I thought that perhaps I shouldn't be afraid of him. He was really quite nice when he smiled. The band and following entourage moved off and grandpa and I went back indoors.

It was nearly time to catch the number 77 Waterworks bus which stopped at the corner of Manor Street and would take us across Agnes Street, Northumberland Street, and Hope Street and finally stop at Shaftesbury Square from where we would walk to just opposite Belfast City Hospital to watch the parade go by.

Everything was ready and we all got aboard the bus. I was not only wearing an orange lily on my new blue frock but I had new white buckskin shoes and white ankle socks. Mum had tied a bunch of my hair up with a white ribbon and told me I looked not so bad – the best compliment I would ever get since generally she reminded me I was so plain she could do nothing with me. Anyway today I was happy, the sun was shining and it was my day. We bundled ourselves onto the bus with all the paraphernalia needed for the day out. Grandpa was allowed to take me upstairs to the front of the bus as a special treat and I watched people with all their day out things getting on the bus until it was full to bursting. At Shaftesbury Square we all tumbled out and set off up Bradbury Place to our chosen spot on the Lisburn Road.

We settled ourselves on travelling rugs and folding stools and dad told everyone who was sitting or standing near us that it was my birthday. He seemed really proud of me and I was so happy. People around us wished me happy birthday and gave me sweets which I had to save until later. I also had a flag called a Union Jack to wave and my feet tapped and danced to every kind of band that passed by. I got tired sitting on the kerb and grandpa lifted me onto his shoulders and he waved at folk he knew and laughed and swayed to the music. Grandpa wasn't an Orangeman but he knew everybody. My heart was bursting with joy. Half way through the parade the picnic was unpacked and we ate cheese and tomato sandwiches washed down with hot sweet tea. Later dad bought ice cream from a cart nearby and the strawberries that nanna had washed were eaten with mouthfuls of the cold confection.

People were talking about how far it was to the Field and I wondered what happened there. It seemed to be very mysterious and probably a grown- up thing that I didn't need to know about. I often heard things and was told I didn't need to know that. The little boys carrying the banner strings looked hot and a bit tired and I wanted to share my ice-cream and strawberries but mum explained the boys couldn't stop or they wouldn't be able to catch up. Some old men were in black cars and were waving at me as they went past. I guessed they must be very important or perhaps their legs just didn't work too well.

When the parade was almost over a cake and four lighted candles was produced as if by magic and I blew them out with one big puff while everyone told me to make a wish. My wish was that the day wouldn't end and that we could all stay in this happy sunny wonderful place for ever.

As the sound of the last band slipped into the distance my grandmother told me that next year I would be five and too big to be a wee girl perched on Grandpa's shoulders. Next year seemed a long way away and today was just perfect so no need to think about it. We gathered everything up and made our way back to catch the bus home, all a bit dishevelled, my orange lily now wilting on a grubby blue dress. My father was humming the party tunes as he held my hand tightly and steered me towards the bus stop.

That was the last time I believed the Twelfth parade was for my birthday. By the ripe old age of five my childish illusions had been shattered and I became just an ordinary wee girl. But the magic of having a birthday on the Twelfth of July stayed with me. I still watched the parade each year and the sound of the pipes and drums and flute bands playing the Sash my Father Wore were still part of my special day.

The last two years I have been living in Scotland and I hear the sound of the bag-pipes very often. Each time I do my mind flits back to the spectacle of swaying kilts, fluttering banners, orange sashes, flag waving, and foot tapping picnic days on Belfast's Lisburn Road.

This year is my 60th birthday and I am so glad that I can look back on the good days of the Twelfth of July "birthday parade" and an age of innocence when the only thing that parade symbolised was my very happy birthday.

Sylvia Jeffrey, Perthshire

Cavan band parade in Belfast

One of the best memories I have of the Twelfth was in 1967 when I was nine years old. At the time my family lived in a small Protestant community in a country area near Killeshandra, Co Cavan.

My dad and my brother were members of Derrylane Flute Band. My dad usually played the flute but he could also beat the drum. My brother who was then aged eight played the triangles.

One of the members of the band, who was my uncle by marriage, had a brother who lived in Belfast. The band was invited to take part in the Twelfth in Belfast. Imagine a small flute band from the Republic of Ireland taking part in a parade in the city. It was the talk of the area for weeks.

As all the band members were from the farming community plans had to be made to have cows milked either by neighbours or to have the work done before the bus left at 4.30am!

Well, needless to say there was very little sleep the night before. Each year I had attended the Twelfth in Co Fermanagh but not in Belfast. The day finally arrived. My mum and dad were up in the middle of the night to milk the cows and we were all ready for the off on time.

Everyone was so excited and none of us knew what to expect or how long the walk was. A bit different from the walk in Enniskillen.

I can remember my amazement when we reached the motorway. A long straight road with two lanes of traffic going in the same direction with bridges crossing over it. Well I had never seen anything like this before. I remember trying to count the bridges but soon got tired.

The man who was meeting us in Belfast, a Walter Armstrong, had arranged to meet the bus at the end of the motorway to bring us to his home. Unfortunately I do not remember the area of the city but I think it was towards the Shankill area.

When we arrived we were greeted like celebrities. We were divided into small groups and taken to different houses in the area for breakfast. A full cooked breakfast was just what we needed after such a long journey. I can remember how small the houses were, much smaller than our farm house. After breakfast Walter's daughter brought my brother and I to meet some of her friends. But at 8.00am some were not even up. I can recall seeing all the smouldering bonfires on the streets from the night before. Some sight for a girl from the Republic of Ireland.

Shortly afterwards the band formed up and it proceeded around the area to the homes of the different officers of the lodge. Then it proceeded to Carlisle Circus to join the main parade.

Mrs Armstrong brought my mother and I by bus, first of all to the City Hall and then out to Finaghy where my dad's brother George lived. I had never been on a double decker bus before.

Finally we reached my uncle's house in Sicily Park and I had a great time playing with my two cousins. Soon it was time to go down to the Lisburn Road to watch the parade. What a parade. I had never seen anything like it. It just went on for ever. Eventually our band appeared. They all looked tired but we were so proud of them. My brother saw us in the crowd and he smiled at us. When the parade had finished we returned to my uncle's house for some food and a rest. But soon it was time to go back to the Lisburn Road to watch the parade return. Someone was missing from the band, my brother. Mum was so worried. Where was he? What had happened? But all was well. He was unable to walk the return journey. The early start, the long journey and the long walk was just too much for an eight year old. He stayed with us and returned to Mr Armstrong's house on the bus.

When the parade returned to Carlisle Circus we were taken to a hall for food before we started off for home again.

We arrived home in the early hours of the next day, weary but with great memories of the day a small band travelled to the big smoke for the best day of the year. Even today we still talk about the day.

Valerie McMorris, Ballinamallard

Carrying the strings

Pictured with my wife and son

Ihave been in the Order fifty years this year, I have enjoyed every minute of it. I am from an Orange family. My father, grandfather and uncle all were in the Order.

My two brothers, two nephews and my son are in the Order, also my grandson joined the Juniors this year. I am a Past Master in LOL 591 and also LOL 746 where I am now a member. My son is also a Past Master of both lodges. One of the great times I had was when I lived in Antrim. My wife and I papered the first arch in the Steeple. At that time Vanguard had a meeting in Antrim and Jim Molyneaux and Bill Craig were there and they came to see us at work. We also had them at our house for tea after the opening of the arch.

With my father on his last Twelfth

I have walked with the Orange Order since I was a small boy carrying the strings in my late father's Lodge LOL 591. I also enjoyed a day trip on Saturday 16th June 2007 to Dan Winter's cottage. It was a very good day. Mrs Winter welcomed us and gave us a lovely supper. The trip was put on by Ballygarvey LOL 591. I am now 66 years old and hope to see as many more Twelfths as my late father. He was in his 96th year when he was called home.

William Gilmore, Ballymena

The Hills of Carrowdore
and a bright shining Shilling!

"They met on that Twelfth morning as they oft' times did before. And the pipe and drums played William's Sons on the Hills of Carrowdore."

It was just beyond Muckle's Corner at Ballyboley. The two poles dug into the hedges on either side of the road, and the banner straddled between them proclaimed a 'Welcome to the Brethren.'

For a nine-year old who had walked the three miles from Cardy Hill to visit the Twelfth field at Carrowdore, that first sign of the celebrations carried scant meaning.

I had travelled more in curiosity than conviction, and it was difficult for me to fully comprehend just who were the "brethren" who were being welcomed. The line of flags, curling in the morning's gentle breeze, seemed to voice an invitation for me to head on towards the village, and the muffled sounds of drum beat and pipe music added to the mystery which appeared to be unfolding over the hill.

Just before the village a group of men wearing sashes turned out of the Waffisle Road and headed towards Carrowdore.

Stirred by the sight, and roused by the music of the accordion band which preceded them, I eagerly followed behind. Legs, tired by the walk from Cardy, lost their weariness, and I broke into a skip as I was caught up in the cacophony of sound and colour.

Harry McCormick, who went with me to Dunover Public Elementary School, suddenly appeared and joined the march, and soon squads of young people enrolled in our procession of liveliness as we moved along Carrowdore's wide Main Street towards the Orange Hall. Burly men loitered at the doors of the White Horse Inn, while other groups struggled to lift banners and form up behind us for the parade down the village street.

Our position, right at the front of the cavalcade, added a personal feeling of distinction to our occasion, and the small boy, having his first experience of a Twelfth celebration, was carried along in a momentous bubble of reverberation and exhilaration.

The banners rippled round the poles, and I could make out representations of buildings, portraits of stern-looking men and images of biblical stories.

Even now, 60 years later, I can still recall the feeling of intimacy as I stared at Moses peering out from his hiding place among the bulrushes, and a rush of exhilaration rushed over me as I caught a glimpse of the depiction of the magnificent figure of William, sword in hand, as he sat astride his imposing white charger, with the Boyne waters lapping around its hooves.

Around the Orange hall hundreds more were waiting to join in, and I could pick out the familiar names of Cloughey, Ballywalter, Greyabbey, Portaferry and Portavogie as more banners joined in the Pied Piper-like advance on down past the Crommelin School.

The other boys and girls who had latched on to our unofficial parade as strangers on the outskirts of Carrowdore had become bound together in the carnival atmosphere, and, in our own minds, we had all become an intrinsic and natural ingredient of the whole proceedings.

The parade turned off the main road, and, as we moved past the impressive pillars of Carrowdore Castle we all felt an extra flush of prominence and status. We had arrived at the field, and, as the bandsmen and marchers broke up from the ranks, our unauthorised and private group of marchers set off on our own voyage of discovery. It was a lovely sunny day and all around us groups were settling down on the grass to enjoy a rest. Knotted handkerchiefs replaced bowler hats as the men formed their own friendship groups, and pipe smoke drifted above the sound of laughter and chatter.

We youngsters were almost seductively drawn towards the drums abandoned in heaps around the arena. A strong compulsive urge to sample the involvement at first hand made us pick up the drum sticks and indulge in the experience.

We must have been chased from every pile of drums around the field by good-natured shouts of censure before we found ourselves in front of a marquee which had been positioned over on the far side in view of the resplendent Carrowdore Castle.

A row of rather authoritarian-looking men were gathered behind an extensive table, which was suitably draped with the Union Flag.

As we watched one man, who was still wearing his bowler hat, stepped forward and made his way towards a stand with a microphone. After rapping the microphone with his knuckles and counting into it, he started to thank Brother Crommelin for the use of the ground and for supplying the splendid platform.

His words were greeted by applause from those who had gathered around the front of the marquee, and then a minister wearing the distinctive dog-collar behind his sash, stepped forward, and, raising his arms heavenward, invited the gathering to pray.

Our group, prompted by youthful exuberance, strained to find release, but, driven by an upbringing which demanded respect for all things religious, we waited for the minister to finish his invocation before we scampered off to continue our exploration.

The heat, combined with the exertions of the walk, had pushed several of the men into slumber, and once again grumbles of protest drove us to retreat after we had engaged in the somewhat perilous occupation of poking at the sleeping bodies.

We had practically covered the entire expanse when we came across another knot of tents and caravans. We had discovered the ice cream stalls and the sandwich bar.

It was then that I realised that the bright shining shilling which my mother had handed over before I'd left Cardy was missing.

A desperate hunt through the pockets of my trousers revealed nothing more than a rather dirty handkerchief and a few bundles of string which I had intended to use to make a bow or a fishing rod. The shilling was gone!

The others were noisily exchanging their money for ice cream cones and bottles of soda and didn't even notice as I slid away out of their company.

My day had suddenly dipped into disappointment, and, for the first time since I'd reached the banner just beyond Muckle's Corner, my spirits sagged. I couldn't prevent a tear slip down my cheek as I tried to imagine just where my bright shining shilling had escaped from my pocket.

It was then that I noticed the brawny figure of an Orangeman standing looking over me.

"Are you Bob Nash's son?" he asked, in a tone which was friendly and warm. I responded positively and he reached out and, with a firm grip, shook my hand. He had noticed the tear, and, after informing him that my father was still with the Royal Air Force, I found myself telling him about my bright shining shilling. He immediately grabbed my hand again in that vice-like hold and lead me back to the ice cream van.

"Give me the biggest ice cream cone you have," said my new-found friend, "and I'll have one of those miniature Union Flags as well, thank you very much."

He proceeded to push the cone into my grasp, and, after sticking the flag into my jersey, he turned and left, instructing me to tell my father that "Big Davy" had sent his regards.

As if by magic, just as the swallows gather at the end of the summer, the bands regrouped, and the return parade was underway. I found myself back in a group near the head of the line, and I felt even more important than before, since now I had the added pleasure of waving my Union Flag at the crowds gathered on the roads edge. All too soon the line of marchers reached the Orange hall and began to break up.

Banners were unfurled, musical instruments were packed away and tired marchers started to climb on to the buses which stretched in an orderly line right up the Main Street beyond the Tavern Bar.

I turned my head back in the direction of Cardy and by the time I had returned to Ballyboley Corner, all the sights and the sounds of my day at the Twelfth field by the hills of Carrowdore, had been rolled away into a bundle of very happy memories.

Right down through Kerr's Isle and up past Graham's Shop to Cardy Corner I waved my flag, and, although the only spectators this time were the cows and sheep munching the grass in the fields behind the hedges, my imagination carried me back to the hustle, the bustle and the excitement I had enjoyed beside the Hills of Carrowdore.

"Let's toast to King William's memory both now and evermore, not forgetting our Loyal Brethren and our own sweet Carrowdore."

Dennis Nash, Newtownards